MW00627873

18 WORDS TO LIVE BY

A Father's Wisdom
on What Matters Most

KENT SANDERS

NEW ATHENS
PUBLISHING

18 Words to Live By: A Father's Wisdom on What Matters Most

© 2022 by Kent Sanders

All rights reserved. No part of this book may be reproduced, stored in a retrieval system, or transmitted in any form or by any means—electronic, mechanical, photocopy, recording, scanning, or other—except for brief quotations in critical reviews or articles, without the prior written permission of the author.

Scripture quotations are from the ESV® Bible (The Holy Bible, English Standard Version®), Copyright © 2001 by Crossway, a publishing ministry of Good News Publishers. Used by permission. All rights reserved.

About New Athens Publishing: The ancient city of Athens was a crossroads for wisdom, storytelling, and learning. The goal of New Athens Publishing is to continue this tradition by creating fresh conversations around timeless ideas.

Printed in the United States of America.

ISBN 9781957189024 (paperback)
ISBN 9781957189000 (hardback)
ISBN 9781957189017 (ebook)

Cover design & layout by Kristi Griffith, GoThumbprint.com.

CONTENTS

PROLOGUE

To Ben on Your 18th Birthday

Dear Ben,

The idea for this book came to me last year when I suddenly realized you were about to turn 18.

That may sound crazy. Who doesn't know their kid is about to turn 18? But ask any parent whose kids have made it past high school, and they will tell you that life has a way of sneaking up on you.

When your child is two or three years old, it seems like school is an eternity away. They want your attention all the time. It's hard to get a moment's peace, especially for parents who are home with their kids all day. But as the years go by and your child gets older, time seems to speed up. It's the strangest thing.

I remember when you started junior high. You were eleven. For your mom and me, your high school years seemed like a long way off. Then when you started high school, I thought, "We still have four years with him." But the time has flown by. One day you were a freshman, and the next day you were a senior.

As I considered what to give you for this milestone birthday, my mind naturally turned to writing a book. I wanted to give you something you can pass on to your own kids someday.

Fathers pass down things to their kids. It's what we do. We can pass down money, family heirlooms, or property. We can also pass on personality traits, good genes if we have them (somehow I missed out on the "full head of hair" gene), or a family reputation.

All of these gifts can make your life easier or more enjoyable. But one gift towers above them all: the gift of wisdom.

A father can give his children all the material things in the world. But if he doesn't teach them how to live, he's robbed them of a blessing that keeps them grounded in a complicated and confusing world.

In this little book, I share 18 essential values to carry with you on life's journey. These will help you become a person of character, a person whom other people trust and admire.

But this book is not just for you. It's also for your children, grandchildren, and great grandchildren. There is a lot of value in learning to think not only five or ten years into the future, but a hundred.

Are my words in this book wise? That's up to you to decide. Only time will tell whether I have given you something ultimately of value. All I can do is share what I know to be true.

You can read this book and gain some insights now. But in twenty or thirty years, your perspective will be different. You will be older and wiser. I trust you will find a way to pass on your wisdom to your children, just as I pass on mine to you now.

One day many decades from now, long after I am gone, one of your great grandkids will be moving some boxes or cleaning out their basement. They will stumble across a dusty little book titled *18 Words to Live By* and notice that the author's name is Sanders. Recognizing a family name, they will flip it open and realize it was written for you.

As they read what I'm going to share with you, I hope they will take away a little bit of wisdom. But far more than that, I hope they will remember the person you had become and how you impacted their life.

Most of all, I hope these 18 words will be much more than chapters in a short book. I hope they will carry you to greater success far beyond what I will ever achieve.

I am so proud of you, not only for the person you are, but for the one you are becoming. I love you and will always be here for you. Happy 18th birthday.

Love,
Dad

April 11, 2022

INTRODUCTION

"Deep and simple is far more essential
than shallow and complex."
— MISTER ROGERS

I was born in 1974 and grew up in a double-wide trailer five miles outside of Potosi, Missouri. Potosi is a little town in the southeastern part of the state. Like most Missouri natives, I grew up around people who like to keep things straightforward and simple. There's a reason it's called the "Show Me" state.

I was a pop culture junkie as a kid. I loved Saturday morning cartoons (I was obsessed with *Battle of the Planets*), sitcoms (*Diff'rent Strokes* was the bomb), and cheesy shows like *That's Incredible!* But my entertainment options were somewhat limited.

We had an antenna on the roof of our trailer because we lived too far out in the country to get cable. When I would visit my cousins who lived in town, I was always jealous because *they* had cable. I grew up wondering what it was like to live in such luxury that you had HBO!

By contrast, our antenna only piped in seven channels: ABC, CBS, NBC, PBS, KPLR (a local St. Louis station), KNLC (a local religious station), and in my high school years, FOX.

It was a simpler time that required you to pay attention. If you wanted to watch *The Wizard of Oz* or *Rudolph the Red-Nosed Reindeer* when they came around on CBS once a year, you'd better make sure you were subscribed to *TV Guide* or you'd miss it. By contrast, today we have the internet and countless streaming services to offer almost any program on demand.

What has happened to TV stations has also happened to life in general. Things are more complicated. There are lots more options. We have endless choices about where to live, how to spend our time and money, who we hang out with, and what kind of career to build.

This is both a blessing and a curse. Too many options can make you emotionally paralyzed. You spend half your life wondering what direction to go, and by the time you've decided, the ride is almost done.

Is there a better way to live? Is there a compass that can guide us in good times and bad? Is there a clear way forward through the fog and confusion of modern life?

THE VALUE OF VALUES

People have answered the previous question in different ways. The Stoics have the Four Virtues. People of faith have the Ten Commandments. Individuals in recovery have the Twelve Steps. Professional organizations have a Code of Ethics.

It's important to know what you stand for. When life gets confusing and you don't know how to respond, what internal compass will guide you?

All this talk of principles and ethics sounds lofty, but it's quite useful to live by a set of values. It makes life easier. Rather than being a set of dry, dusty ideals, your values should make your life better in a tangible way.

Your values should bring you peace. They should help you be successful. They should elevate others. They should improve your relationships and make the world a better place. Your values should make your life more, well, valuable!

I originally envisioned *18 Words to Live By* as a fun little book to give my son for his 18th birthday. I'm a ghostwriter and author coach, so the project seemed simple enough. But as I started thinking about which 18 words I would choose, I realized it would be harder than I thought.

The effort was worth it. Putting this book together reinforced the values I try to live by. It also helped me see where I continue to fall short. It was a humbling yet gratifying experience.

WE ALL NEED WISDOM

Since I originally wrote this for my son Ben, you may be wondering if this book is for you, too. The answer is a resounding *yes*.

Why? Because we all need to be reminded of the basics sometimes. Whether you're a teenager, single mother, senior citizen, CEO, veteran, college student, or somewhere in between, you'll find a lot of encouragement and inspiration for your journey in these pages.

It doesn't matter who you are. You're never too old for a father's wisdom.

I've designed the book to give you a flexible reading experience. It is short enough to read in one or two sittings but you can also dip in and out of it as needed. Each chapter only takes a few minutes to read, and the print version is intentionally small so you can carry it with you.

18 Words to Live By is a little handbook for life. As a writer, I've tried to make it fun to read. But the teacher in me also wants you to apply what you learn. That's why I've included a discussion guide at the end of the book to help you put the material into practice.

I don't claim to offer infallible wisdom from on high. These are not the *18 Virtues*, the *18 Commandments*, or the *18 Steps*. They are simply a few words from an imperfect father trying to pass on a few bits of wisdom.

As I think about the endless array of entertainment options today, maybe it wasn't so bad having just a few TV channels as a kid. There is a certain beauty in focusing on the essentials.

This book has reminded me what matters most in life. I hope these 18 simple words give you clarity about what matters most in your life, too.

I. RESPONSIBILITY

Take Charge of Your Life

"You have power over your mind – not outside events.
Realize this, and you will find strength."
—MARCUS AURELIUS

I taught at a small college in north St. Louis for many years. My commute took about thirty minutes. I had to make sure I took everything with me that I needed for the day, including my computer, phone, books, and class folders.

The most important item was my set of keys. I had to go through three doors to get to my office: an outside door, a door that led upstairs to faculty offices, then my office door. Without my keys, I couldn't even get into the building.

I would occasionally forget to take them with me. This was a big problem in the winter. I would have to stand at the door in the cold, knocking until somebody let me in. It's pretty hard to get inside if you don't have the key to open the door.

That's a good analogy for life. Every day, there are millions of people standing at the door to success, hoping someone will let them in because they can't find the key.

THE MASTER KEY

You need many qualities in order to lead a successful life. This book is filled with 18 of them. But one quality, one master key, opens the door to all the rest.

It has nothing to do with where you were born or how smart you are. It's not about your looks, personality, or natural talent. It doesn't matter who your parents are or what connections you may or may not have.

All of those can be helpful. However, they pale in comparison to the most important key to success: responsibility.

That is what this whole book is about. You will lead a successful life based on whether you take responsibility for your own success. More than anything else, taking responsibility will account for your happiness and success in every area of your life.

We hear the word responsibility tossed around a lot. But what does it mean? It's made of two words: response and ability. It is the ability to respond.

Contrast this with the word react. When you react to something, it puts you on the defensive. You let external events determine your emotional state.

But responding is different. It puts you in the driver's seat. You own your response. You have response ability.

Successful people do their best to respond to life instead of reacting to it. They determine their own destiny. They don't passively wait around for someone to give them opportunities. Instead, they actively seek them out.

In the 2008 film The Dark Knight, Gotham's District Attorney Harvey Dent carries a two-headed coin. His motto is, "I make my own luck." (That, plus "I want to kill Batman because he put me in a situation where my chair tipped over and I burned half my face off in a puddle of acid," but it doesn't have quite the same ring.)

After Harvey Dent becomes the criminal Two-Face, he scars one side of the coin to match his face. He flips the coin whenever he has to decide the fate of others.

He has gone from "making his own luck" to leaving everything to chance.

You get to decide what kind of coin you carry with you in life. Do you make your own luck by taking responsibility? Or do you leave your fate—and the fate of others—to chance by failing to accept responsibility?

MAKE A DECISION

The Lewis & Clark Trail is one of the most popular hiking spots near St. Louis. It snakes through the woods with an amazing diversity of wildlife and stunning views from bluffs overlooking the Missouri River.

You have two decisions to make when you hike this trail. The first is which path to take. Will you go with the shorter 5.5-mile Clark Trail or the longer 8.5-mile Lewis Trail? You must also decide if you are going to hike in a clockwise or counterclockwise direction.

I have hiked every version of this trail over the years. But I confess that more than once, I have stood in the parking lot staring at the trail for ten minutes, trying to decide which path to take and which direction to go. I wasted precious daylight trying to make the "right" decision when in fact there was no right decision. All decisions were equally good because they all put me on the trail.

Sometimes life presents you with several good options, and there is no clear answer. When this happens, make a list of the pros and cons. Then make your decision and move forward.

Sometimes we don't make decisions because we're afraid to be wrong. We don't want to accept responsibility for a bad decision. When you feel paralyzed by a decision, just pick a path and start moving. You can always backtrack and start over. The answer will reveal itself as you go.

As Dory said in Finding Nemo, "Just keep swimming, just keep swimming." Who would have thought an animated fish could be so wise?

DON'T PLAY THE VICTIM

Lots of people play the victim role their whole life. And why not? It's much easier to blame your problems on others instead of taking responsibility.

Can people, institutions, and random events cause you trouble and heartache? Of course. But even in the worst of circumstances, you can still choose how you respond to any situation.

Henry David Thoreau said, "The mass of men lead lives of quiet desperation." Where does desperation come from? It comes from a sense of having no hope for a better future. If you always see yourself as a victim, you have no hope because you don't think you have any power.

Where does power come from? It comes from taking responsibility for your life. Whatever you are facing, look around and ask yourself, "What can I do to improve my situation?" There is always something you can do to make things better.

When you choose to act, you are empowered.

In Spider-Man lore, Peter Parker's Uncle Ben famously told him, "With great power comes great responsibility." The opposite is also true—with great responsibility comes great power.

When you choose your response, when you "act upon" life rather than being "acted upon," great things will happen. You become the captain of your own ship. You get to determine how successful you want to become.

Responsibility is the master key that unlocks your life's possibilities. Don't ever lose it, or you'll be left standing out in the cold.

2. COURAGE

Act in the Face of Fear

"If it scares you, it might be a good thing to try."
—SETH GODIN

One chilly night in January 1988, I sat with a few of my buddies on the bleachers in the junior high gym. I was in the eighth grade, and we were there for the winter dance. I was all decked out in my dress clothes and a gray wool jacket my older brother let me borrow.

A girl came up to me out of nowhere and said, "Cindy wants to dance with you." Cindy (not her real name) was the younger sister of my brother's girlfriend. Cindy was also in sixth grade.

I had a bit of a crush on her and was flattered that she wanted to dance with me. However, I was afraid of what my eighth-grade friends would think. There are certain things you don't do in life, and dancing with a sixth grader was one of them. (At least, that's what I thought at the time).

I asked Cindy's friend to tell her no. I didn't want to be embarrassed in front of my friends.

Maybe you have been in a similar situation. It's the easiest thing in the world to stay planted on the bleachers because you're afraid. But the world is full of dance floors calling you to get up and move. The situation might be a job interview, an opportunity to collaborate with someone you respect, or a romantic interest. We all do the same thing when we face a scary situation.

We're afraid of what others might think, so we step back into the shadows and never seize what we want.

NAMING YOUR FEARS

A few years ago, one of my writing friends got in touch. He was working on a project related to fear. He asked if I would name some of the fears I have as a writer.

I said I would help and started making a list. Once I got started, I couldn't stop. I was amazed at how many things I was afraid of. Here are a few fears I wrote down:

- *I am never going to build an audience and make any money from this.*

- *People are only humoring me and being nice.*

- *I'm not that great.*

- *Nobody respects me.*

- *I am never going to be as successful as [well-known author].*

- *I wonder if people would respect me more if I had a book deal with a publisher.*

- *I have become what I always feared: a middle-aged guy with thinning hair who needs to lose about 40 lbs. and has barely had any success. I have become* that guy *whom everybody is nice to on the surface, but they make fun of once he has left the room.*

There is great power in naming your fears. Once I began to write them down, I saw how ridiculous most of them were. In the few years since I made that list, many of those fears have been proven wrong.

Fear grows when we keep it in the dark. When you drag your fears into the light and write them down, you see them for what they really are: distractions that keep you from moving forward.

Whenever you feel afraid, give this exercise a try. It only takes a few minutes, but it's powerful.

WHAT'S THE WORST THAT COULD HAPPEN?

When I feel afraid, I sometimes ask myself, "What's the worst that could happen?" This question takes the wind out of fear's sails. When you define your fear and take it to its logical conclusion, it removes the power fear has over you.

My insurance agent invited me to a networking luncheon when I started building my business. I knew it was a good opportunity to make some connections. However, I was nervous because he was the only person there I would know. I'm an introvert who feels awkward introducing myself to strangers.

I arrived fifteen minutes early and chatted with the guy taking tickets. I used the restroom and then saw a couple of people talking. I didn't know either one of them and I didn't want to barge in on their conversation. So I set down my notebook on a nearby table and just stood there awkwardly.

I thought to myself, *Why don't you sit down and just play on your phone? Pretend like you're doing something important.* But I knew that was lame, so I did what every self-respecting businessperson does when feeling socially awkward.

I hid in the bathroom.

This seemed weird since I had just used the bathroom ninety seconds earlier, but I went back in anyway. I washed my hands again for no reason, then checked my personal email. And my business email. And social media. Then I looked up the latest Star Wars movie news and checked my favorite news site.

After five minutes, I couldn't think of anything else to do, so I stood there looking at myself in the mirror. I had three thoughts.

Thought #1: *You should wear a suit jacket more often. It makes you look more professional!*

Thought #2: S*top sucking in your gut. You're going to need to breathe at some point in the next hour.*

Thought #3: *Okay, Kent. Time to man up. You're a pro. What's the worst that could happen? Time to face your fears.*

I gathered my wits, stepped out of the bathroom, and pretended I was outgoing. And you know what? Pretty soon I actually *felt* outgoing and was genuinely enjoying myself.

We all want to hide in the bathroom at times. But there comes a time when you must look at yourself in the mirror, set your fears aside, and go shake some hands.

IT'S TIME TO DANCE

A few years ago, I attended my nephew's wedding. It was beautiful ceremony. The reception featured a dance, which was a lot of fun.

Partway through the reception, Ed Sheeran's song "Thinking Out Loud" began to play. I'm not a good dancer. I'm a drummer and guitar player, but the rhythm I can produce in my hands and feet doesn't translate to the rest of my body.

For just a moment, I became a scared 8th-grade kid sitting on the bleachers. But then I remembered I'm not that kid anymore. I stood up and asked my wife, "Care to dance?"

What about you? Can you hear the music? Do you feel the rhythm?

Your song is playing. It's time to get up and dance.

3. EMPATHY

See the World Through Another's Eyes

"In all my work what I try to say is that as human beings
we are more alike than we are unalike."
—MAYA ANGELOU

You've heard the advice that you should walk a mile in someone else's shoes. But there is a simple reason why it's so hard: nobody else's shoes fit your feet.

You have a unique perspective. You see the world in a certain way. You have our own personality, experiences, gifts, interests, goals, and history. You are a singularly unique individual.

It's hard to look at life from another person's perspective. It's hard to imagine their pain and see yourself in their situation. It's hard to be empathetic. And yet understanding another person's point of view is one of the most important skills you can ever develop.

Humans have always gathered in tribes. We are suspicious of people who don't think like us, act like us, or look like us.

But over the last decade, that suspicion has grown into outright hostility. The most common way to deal with disagreements is to call people out on social media or "cancel" them (as if that even makes sense). Social media has made it possible for anyone to have a voice, even if they express a hurtful viewpoint or are just plain evil. We have lost the ability to "agree to disagree," to listen empathetically, and to be friends with people without having to agree on everything.

How can we find our way back?

THE LOST ART OF LISTENING

In his famous book *The 7 Habits of Highly Effective People*, Steven Covey says, "Seek first to understand, then to be understood." It's hard to do this because our first impulse is to try to get the other person to hear us first.

Have you ever sat in a coffee shop and watched two people talking? Here is what you will see 99% of the time. One person will be talking, and the other will be anxiously awaiting their turn to speak. When the first person is through, they jump in with their response. Then the cycle repeats.

This is a microcosm of the world today. Everyone is so busy talking that nobody is listening.

I taught public speaking for many years in college. One of the first lessons of the semester involved active listening. All communication involves as much listening as it does speaking. To illustrate how hard it was to listen carefully, I lined up all the students in a row to play the "telephone game."

Here is how it works: the first person whispers a sentence into the next person's ear. Then it's whispered down the line, person to person, until the final person reveals what they heard. I usually began with a complicated sentence like this one: "The sun is a giant thermonuclear reactor that is 27 million degrees at its core." By the time it got to the end, the sentence was so garbled you could barely recognize it.

During the game, a student would often overhear what their friend was whispering into the next person's ear. They would exclaim, "That's not what I said!" There clearly had been a gap in their communication.

That was the whole point of the game: to illustrate that it takes a lot of hard work to listen. In a world where no one stops talking, how can you start to become a better listener?

It begins with love.

THE LOST ART OF LOVE

Love gets a bad rap these days. We have reduced it to a sappy sentiment hauled out for romantic comedies and Valentine's Day. If you were to stand up and proclaim that love could solve an awful lot of the world's problems, nobody would take you seriously.

But what if love *was* the answer?

At its core, loving another person means you value them. You ascribe worth to them. You assume that every person you meet has something valuable to offer no matter who they are.

But here is the key: you must be willing to listen and receive it.

When I was in junior high band, there was a kid named Doug (not his real name). Everybody made fun of him because he was socially awkward and talked funny. I confess that I joined in the ridicule a few times.

I wish I could go back in time and talk to my junior high self. I'd tell that arrogant kid that everybody deserves respect, that Doug was a good guy who badly needed a friend.

Sometimes I wonder what I missed by not being a real friend to Doug. What if I could have seen past Doug's awkwardness and offered my friendship? I suspect that I would have made a great friend.

OUR NUMBER-ONE NEED

Let me share a simple way to love people more. Think of a person who irritates you. Maybe it's that relative who never stops talking or the guy at work who is a loudmouth. Maybe it's your next-door neighbor who won't stop their dogs from barking.

Picture that person in your mind. Then ask yourself, "Do I really value this person? Do I care about their welfare? Do I want their best for them?" The answer will reveal what's in your heart.

The more you ask these questions about the people in your life, the more you will come to love and value them. You will listen more. You will develop more empathy.

One of my favorite quotes is attributed to Plato: "Be kind, for everyone you meet is fighting a hard battle." Every time you engage with another person, you can safely assume they are going through something difficult.

You can't change the world, but you can change the world for one person. How? By trying to see life from their perspective and making them feel understood, loved, and valued. This is our number-one emotional need as humans.

If you can master this skill, you will have more friends than you can possibly imagine.

4. GENEROSITY

Give From the Overflow

"We make a living by what we get.
We make a life by what we give."
—WINSTON CHURCHILL

One of the best parts of my job as a writer is the opportunity to collaborate with amazing leaders and thinkers. In the fall of 2020, I had the opportunity to collaborate with authors David Hancock and Bobby Kipper on their book *Performance Driven Giving: The Roadmap to Unleashing the Power of Generosity in Your Life.* The book's main idea is that giving helps you perform better in every part of your life.

We included interviews with a dozen business leaders in the book. Many of them were financially successful. Even though they came from various backgrounds, these leaders had one thing in common: they are all generous.

This may come as a surprise to many people, but it is rare to find a wealthy person who is not generous.

Generosity is not really about money. Money is just a container for energy and a means of exchanging value. A generous person has an abundance mindset. They believe there is more than enough to go around. They also believe that value (and therefore, money) can be created out of thin air.

Contrast this with someone who has a poverty minds et. They believe success and blessings are scarce resources. They are convinced you must hoard what you have because there is only so much to go around.

Which one has more fun in life? Which one helps more people? Which one is probably more successful? You can probably guess.

LIVING IN THE OVERFLOW

For the most part, life gives you what you're seeking.

If you believe everyone is out to get you, that successful people must have cheated to get where they are, and that every day is going to be horrible . . . that is what you will find.

On the other hand, if you believe good things will happen to you, that people are mostly good and loving, and that opportunity lies around every corner . . . that is what you will find.

Some people say, "When life gives you lemons, make lemonade." I say, "When life gives you lemons, gather some generous friends to help you make lemonade, then share it with the neighborhood."

Most people think to themselves, "I'll wait until I have more to share. Then I'll be generous." This is backward thinking. The more you give, the more successful you will be in life. But success doesn't come from the giving—it comes from the underlying qualities that cause you to give in the first place.

Those qualities include love, gratitude, and joy. A person with those qualities will always be a giver. They are headed for success. They see every day as a blessing, and they are happy to share what they have with others.

TEN WAYS TO BE GENEROUS

Generosity is not just about money. It's an orientation toward life that affects your daily actions. Here are ten simple ways to be generous in your everyday life.

1. **Open the door for people.** It's such a basic gesture. A person who holds the door shows they value people. They put other people's interests ahead of their own. If you ever conduct a job interview, pay

attention to which candidates hold the door for others. It will tell you a lot about their character.

2. **Promote services and products you love.** If there is something you love, tell people about it. Leave reviews online. Share it with your audience. If something has helped you, other people will love it, too.

3. **Support your friends' businesses.** As a writer, I love buying, gifting, and promoting books my author friends have written. But this principle works for every business. Your friends will love you for it.

4. **Share positive gossip.** It's the easiest thing in the world to spread sordid news about people. Why not turn this principle on its head? Tell people all about the good things your family, friends, and colleagues have done.

5. **Do more than is expected.** Most people only do what is required. But as a generous person, always add a little extra touch. Go the extra mile, and give more value than you've been paid for. It will come back to you in the form of referrals, goodwill, and loyalty.

6. **Give other people credit.** The best leaders give credit to others who helped them succeed. You will never accomplish anything worthwhile by yourself. Make sure to brag on people who have played a role in your success.

7. **Help someone financially.** When you hear of someone in need, send money. It doesn't need to be a lot. A few years ago, I had to borrow $300 from my dad to take a ghostwriting course. That money changed my life, and I was grateful for his generosity. When I tried to pay him back, he wouldn't let me. You will be surprised how much your financial generosity means to people when they are going through a hard time.

8. **Make introductions between people.** I always pay attention to the needs of people in my network. If they need something specific, I connect them with someone who can help. These connections can come back to help you in surprising ways.

9. **Send unexpected gifts.** One of the best ways to build loyalty and goodwill is to send books, cards, and other random gifts. We never grow out

of the excitement of getting stuff in the mail. I frequently send items to friends and clients to show my appreciation. These gifts make a memorable impression.

10. **Leave generous tips.** Don't be one of those people who pulls out a calculator when the bill comes to ensure they don't leave a penny over 15%. Here's a simple rule I follow: for every $10 of the bill, I leave a $2 tip, plus extra. This guarantees a minimum tip of 20–25%. I often leave more. I also carry a money clip so I can leave cash tips, which servers appreciate.

These might seem like simple suggestions, but they will make a world of difference to the person receiving them. You will enjoy it just as much as they do—probably even more.

GENEROSITY ALSO MEANS RECEIVING

Despite all the good things associated with generosity, I must be honest and mention its dark side. Generous people frequently have a hard time receiving.

Earlier, I mentioned the interviews I conducted for *Performance Driven Giving*. The most surprising takeaway for me was learning that many of the people I interviewed have a hard time receiving. They love giving but find it hard to accept help from others.

Generosity isn't a one-way street. It's important to bless others, but you must also allow them to bless *you*. When you refuse someone's help or gifts, you block them from expressing their generosity.

It's all about living in the flow. When you let the blessings of generosity flow into your life and out to others, you will be amazed at the joy it will bring.

5. CREATIVITY

Partner with Great Collaborators

"Creativity is God's gift to us. Using our creativity
is our gift back to God."
—Julia Cameron

Creativity is like a good cup of coffee: everybody wants it, it takes time to brew, and it's best enjoyed in the company of a good friend.

I've always been obsessed with the creative process, especially when it comes to movies. I'm the geek who always watches the behind-the-scenes documentaries and loves learning how things are made.

One of the most fascinating aspects of filmmaking is that no movie gets made alone. In a typical Hollywood movie production, there are hundreds, often thousands, of people required to take an idea from a story concept all the way to a finished movie.

Everyone involved in the movie must support each other. The screenwriter, director, producer, actors, lighting and sound people, construction crew, special effects artists, costume designers, and countless others have to coordinate their efforts for a common cause. Otherwise, the movie won't get made.

This is a great lesson for all of us who do creative work. (And by the way, *all* work is creative work.) We accomplish more when we partner with great collaborators.

For several years, I focused on the topic of creativity in my writing and teaching. I also hosted a podcast called *Born to Create*. One of my previous books is titled *The Artist's Suitcase: 26 Essentials for the Creative Journey*. I created good material, but one of my glaring errors was that I did not emphasize the importance of collaboration enough.

As a writer, blogger, and podcaster, that was okay since I could do those things mostly on my own. But one of the main lessons I have learned as a ghostwriter is that it's nearly impossible to create amazing work by yourself.

INDEPENDENCE IS OVERRATED

I believe in independence. As an American, I appreciate that we are a sovereign nation. I am grateful that we fought the Revolutionary War for our freedom. I am also a member of a fellowship of churches that values independence. Each church is its own entity and can make its own decisions without interference from a headquarters.

Personal freedom is one of my highest core values. I've always loved working alone, and my parents raised me to be independent. I can take care of myself.

That is all well and good. But when it comes to your creative life, independence is highly overrated. You need the input, advice, ideas, and sanity of other people to help keep you grounded and accountable.

Take the process of creating a book. Even though you are writing the book as the author, you might be working with a developmental editor to refine and organize your ideas. You might have the help of beta readers who can give you early feedback. You will have at least one editor check for errors and proofread the final manuscript. You will also have a graphic designer for the cover and interior layout.

You might also put together a book launch team to help spread the word. And finally, you will ask friends, fans, and readers to buy, read, share, and leave reviews for the book.

That's a lot of effort for just one book! But it's only one example. You can apply the same principles to any creative work.

Independence has its advantages. It's good to be self-sufficient. But you severely limit your success when you only focus on what you can do by yourself.

Dependence is not always healthy, either. You never want to put yourself in a situation where you rely entirely on one employer, client, or partner as the single source of your livelihood or success.

The key is *interdependence*. It is an approach where you rely on others, they rely on you, and you make each other better than you could ever be on your own. Think of the world's greatest creative collaborations and how each person enhanced the other.

Would the Beatles have created some of the best music of all time if Paul McCartney had not teamed up with John Lennon? Would the *Star Wars* films have changed Hollywood history if John Williams had not teamed up with George Lucas? Would Apple have grown into such a valuable company if Steve Jobs had not teamed up with Steve Wozniak?

The answer is a clear no.

Interdependence is not only the best approach to creativity. It is also a lot more fun.

WHAT TO LOOK FOR IN A COLLABORATOR

Over the last couple of years, I have been working on a parable-style book about the writing life. To help me learn about storytelling, I spent a lot of time analyzing several great movies. If you carefully watch the first ten minutes of *Raiders of the Lost Ark*, *Chinatown*, and *Die Hard*, you learn a lot of information about the main characters and what they want.

I had been struggling to figure out the best way to introduce the main character in my book. So I sat down with my wife Melanie, who is a much more gifted storyteller than me. I spent a few minutes talking through the first act of my story. Then within thirty seconds, she diagnosed what was wrong and suggested a brilliant fix.

I encourage you to seek collaborators for your creative projects. It's hard to find people you trust, especially if a project is very personal to you. However, a great collaborator will not only help you make a better final product. They will also encourage and support you.

What should you look for in a creative partner? I suggest these five qualities.

1. **A positive spirit.** You want to work with people who are optimistic and cheerful. No Debbie Downers allowed here.

2. **Curiosity about life.** Stay away from people who think they know everything. The best creative partners are students of life. They ask questions. They are humble. They are relentlessly curious.

3. **Good chemistry.** Do you click with the person? Do you have fun together? Don't overlook this element. If you don't have the same vibe, the partnership will not work well.

4. **Willingness to take a risk.** All good art involves risk. You are creating something new. You are testing out new ideas. Make sure your collaborator is willing to step into the unknown and take a risk.

5. **Desire to help you succeed.** They understand that the greatest success is helping others succeed. When one partner wins, everyone wins.

You should not only look for these qualities in others. You must have them, too. After all, people will be looking for *you* to be a great collaborator. It's a two-way street.

No matter what type of job or business you have, you

will always need to work with great creative partners. It is almost impossible to be successful on your own. Seek out partnerships where you can help others and they can help you.

Just like a great cup of coffee, that is the perfect recipe for a creative brew.

6. AUTHENTICITY

Get Comfortable in Your Own Skin

"Before I can tell my life what I want to do with it,
I must listen to my life telling me who I am."
—PARKER PALMER

A few years ago, I had the rare opportunity to see *It's a Wonderful Life* at the movie theater. It has been one of my favorite movies for many years. The movie tells the story of George Bailey, a young man with big plans who never gets to leave the small town of Bedford Falls. He is too busy taking care of others to pursue his dreams.

Over the years, we see George become frustrated and irritable. He slaves away at the Building & Loan, a small company his father created. George feels responsible for keeping it going, even years after his father's death.

The second half of the movie features an alternate timeline where George gets to see what Bedford Falls would have been like without him. He learns that even though he never "chased his dreams," he still made a big impact on many people's lives.

It's a Wonderful Life is a classic because it reminds us that relationships and community are important. But what might have happened if George had left Bedford Falls?

What if he had taken a risk and bucked other people's expectations? What if he had stepped out of his father's shadow and focused on his own goals and dreams? What if he had been true to himself?

What if George Bailey had lived authentically?

We'll never know the answer since *It's a Wonderful Life* is just a movie. But your life is not a movie. You're a real person with real ambitions. If you are not true to yourself, if you are not comfortable in your own skin, you put yourself in danger of being another George Bailey.

There is only one way to avoid this life of misery and unlock your potential. You must embrace who you are instead of running away from it.

EMBRACE YOUR GIFTS

I love Brad Paisley's music. He is one of the world's finest guitarists. I'm a guitar player, too, yet I know I'll never be as successful as him. He started playing guitar as a kid and has devoted his life to his craft. So I remain content with my average level of guitar skill.

There are areas where I have zero talent, such as sports or dancing. I will never be great in those areas no matter how hard I try. My mind and body are simply not wired that way. I could spend two hours per day working on those skills over the next decade, and I will never be world-class.

However, as a young man I realized I had a natural gift for words and language. I loved to write. People encouraged me in that gift, so I continued to work on it. Rather than fighting it, I embraced writing and have been fortunate to build a career out of it.

A lot of peace and joy comes into your life when you embrace your gifts. There is no reason to fight it. Just accept the way you are wired, then figure out how to be successful at it.

As you grow, you will develop new skills that complement your main set of skills. You will always be happiest when you are moving to the natural rhythm of your gifts.

EMBRACE YOUR SCARS

We all like to show our best side. It's human nature. We try to hide our scars. The problem is that your scars are part of your story. They have made you who you are.

The musician Charlie Puth has a scar on his right eyebrow. Many of his fans assume he shaved it to make an artistic statement. But that's not the case. Charlie was attacked by a dog when he was two years old, and it left a permanent scar. Rather than try to hide it, he has embraced it as part of his image. Some of his devoted fans even shave their right eyebrow to match his look.

Instead of hiding your scars, what if they became your signature feature? What if they inspired others to be authentic, too?

If you're like me, you have made some embarrassing mistakes. You have done some stupid things, thinking you were smart at the time. If so, welcome to the club—the club of being a human being.

You don't need to run from your past. You need to run *toward* it. Embrace your story because it's part of who you are. People relate to failure more than they relate to success. Don't hide your scars.

EMBRACE YOUR APPEARANCE

Most of us are not happy with the way we look. For example, I am a balding middle-aged guy who needs to lose about 40 lbs. Other people might think they're too skinny, too fat, they don't like their hair color, they're too tall, too short, or a hundred other dissatisfactions.

We should strive to be our best both internally and externally. There are things we can do to enhance our appearance and be the healthiest version of ourselves. But all the enhancements in the world can't make you love yourself.

Real change starts with not only *accepting* yourself, but *embracing* yourself. You are a wonderful, beautiful, valuable gem of a person, exactly like you are. No enhancements needed.

You don't need external validation. It's time to start validating yourself. When you embrace who you are inside and out—your gifts, your scars, your appearance—your authenticity will radiate outward to others and change them as well.

Back to *It's a Wonderful Life*. It's no secret that George Bailey was not a successful businessman. He followed in his father's footsteps and stayed in a job where he was miserable because he felt obligated to help the nice people in Bedford Falls.

Did he help people and change lives? Did the people in Bedford Falls love him? Yes and yes.

But imagine what George could have done if he had embraced who he was, if he had been excited about his work and his mission. How much of a bigger impact could he have made not only in Bedford Falls, but far beyond?

7. DISCRETION

Watch Your Words

"Be sure to taste your words before you spit them out."
—Anonymous

I began my freshman year at St. Louis Christian College in Florissant, Missouri, in the fall of 1992. I chose preaching as my college major because I came from a small church in southern Missouri. I assumed preaching was the only viable job option for people who wanted to enter ministry.

I had always felt a calling to become a pastor. To their credit, the people in my home church had supported and encouraged me in my desires. They gave me plenty of opportunities to preach and lead worship. So armed with a healthy sense of spiritual calling and a little bit of confidence, I began my studies to become a preaching pastor.

By the time I finished my junior year, I had been through all the preaching courses. I was pretty confident I knew what constituted a great sermon. My preaching professor, Keith McCaslin, ingrained in us the idea that sermons should only be twenty minutes long. (He was decades ahead of his time since the limit for a TED talk is 18 minutes.)

One Sunday in May 1995, my wife Melanie and I visited a local church led by an older pastor with a reputation for long sermons. The pastor did not disappoint. His sermon was a rambling mess of points and stories that didn't relate to each other.

Later that afternoon, I decided to set the pastor straight. Even though he had been a pastor far longer than I had been alive, I felt the need to give him some guidance. I wrote a long letter telling him how disappointed I was in the sermon. I also generously offered some helpful preaching tips.

Satisfied that I had done the good Lord's work, I dropped the letter in the mail and promptly forgot about it.

Fifteen years went by. In that span of time, I spent eight years as a worship pastor and learned what church leadership was really like. Then I moved back to St. Louis to teach at the same college where I attended.

A few years later, I was invited to be part of a planning committee for a state church convention. That same pastor was part of the group. During one of our meetings, we struck up a conversation. I was sure he would bring up the letter I had written years earlier. But he seemed to have no memory of it. Either that, or he didn't realize I was the one who wrote it.

I felt ashamed for writing that letter years earlier. That type of thing was out of character for me then, and still is today. But in a moment of arrogance as a know-it-all college kid, I felt the need to correct a pastor who was simply a little off his game that day we visited.

They say, "Sticks and stones may break my bones, but words can never hurt me." That is the biggest lie in the history of the world. Words can do incredible damage.

I'm sure my letter to that pastor was hurtful and discouraging. To his credit, he had the self-discipline and maturity to not reply. He used discretion when it came to his words. I wish I had done the same.

In the years since, I have tried to learn from his example and not repeat the same mistake.

THE VALUE OF HAVING NO OPINION

The internet and social media have given us many benefits. Now everyone has a voice and can connect with like-minded people around the world. Unfortunately, that also means everyone has an opinion about everything and is not afraid to share it.

I've never understood why some people are so opinionated. Strong opinions should be reserved for topics where you have deep, intimate knowledge and experience. What is the point of having opinions about things you know little about?

Being opinionated also kills curiosity. A curious, inquisitive person is always seeking knowledge and new perspectives. He or she assumes that there is always something they don't know. Therefore, it's best to reserve judgment and speak in probabilities rather than absolutes.

This is why arguments about religion and politics are almost always a waste of time. (Did you notice I used the word *almost* as a way to avoid giving an absolute rule?) It is impossible to know all the facts of any given issue.

Plus, nobody ever changed their mind as a result of an argument. Arguments make people defensive, and defensive people dig in their heels and hold to their point of view even if they don't believe what they're saying.

Nobody ever said human beings were rational. We do almost everything out of emotion rather than logic. Therefore, it's usually best to keep your opinions to yourself as a way to prevent unnecessary conflict.

I like to be a chameleon on most issues. It's fun to keep people guessing where you stand. In the musical *Hamilton*, Alexander Hamilton frequently makes fun of Aaron Burr for supposedly being wishy-washy and never committing to an issue. Meanwhile, Hamilton has no problem sharing his opinions about anything and everything. His hot temper often got him into trouble.

It's worth noting which one of them got shot.

The most powerful three words in the English language are "I love you." The second most powerful three words are "I don't know." I encourage you to use them often.

THE VALUE OF STAYING NEUTRAL

One of my favorite books is *The 48 Laws of Power* by Robert Greene. The genius of the book is that it reveals how people actually operate in real life.

My favorite principle is Law 4: "Always Say Less Than Necessary." Greene argues that the more you say, the more likely you are to say something foolish. Therefore, it is wise to rein in your words instead of shooting off at the mouth.

This principle has served me well. I am a quiet, reserved person who keeps out of other people's arguments whenever possible.

A number of years ago I worked for a non-profit organization that served thousands of people. I enjoyed working there and felt called to be part of its mission. However, one year things took a turn for the worse when several employees got involved in a complicated conflict situation connected with another influential organization.

The trouble was that I liked a lot of these people even though they were on different sides of the issues. The ongoing conflict was beginning to take an emotional toll on our whole organization, not to mention the damage it was doing to our reputation with outsiders.

Privately, I agreed with a lot of the concerns the employees were voicing. But I was not willing to insert myself into a conflict that was not mine to fight. Plus, I did not have the power or authority to do anything about it.

Therefore, I kept my mouth shut. If others wanted to speak out publicly, that was their choice. But I was not going to endanger my reputation, and perhaps my employment, by getting ensnared in the situation.

This was especially true since I did not have access to all the facts. I was only hearing certain sides of each issue. Therefore, in some of these cases, I had not resolved in my own mind who I thought was "right" or "wrong." It wasn't that simple. It is dangerous to publicly declare your verdict about issues when you have only heard one side of the argument.

As Proverbs 26:17 says, "Whoever meddles in a quarrel not his own is like one who takes a passing dog by the ears." If you insert yourself into an argument, it is inevitable that you will upset one side or the other. If you do this sort of thing regularly, you will develop a reputation as a dramatic person who likes conflict.

Most people like to avoid conflict, so they distance themselves from drama. Therefore, make sure to measure your words. As much as is it possible, don't get involved in other people's battles unless absolutely necessary.

When you use discretion, it doesn't mean you're weak. It means you're wise.

8. PRESENCE

Wherever You Are, Be There

"The greatest gift that you can give to others is the gift
of unconditional love and acceptance."
—BRIAN TRACY

Ten years ago I had a dream that has haunted me
ever since.

In my dream, I was sitting at my aunt's kitchen table
with several family members. My grandfather was also
there, even though he died in 1991.

Someone, I don't remember who, explained that we
had been given a great gift. We had the chance to bring
back my Grandpa for one more day. In the logic of my
dream, everyone could bring back a loved one from the
grave, but just for a day—one final chance to spend time
with them and say goodbye.

That's all I remember about the dream. It was short,
just one brief scene, but I've thought about it a hundred

times since then. I've often wondered how I would spend one last day with my Grandpa if given the chance.

I grew up in southern Missouri and lived next door to Grandpa. He loved to hunt with Dad. But I didn't enjoy hunting as a kid. I can only remember going squirrel hunting with Dad and Grandpa once.

As a young boy, I didn't grasp that hunting wasn't about guns or animals. It was about spending time with my family. All I could see was getting up early and trudging out into the cold woods to sit for a few hours.

But if I could go back in time and spend one last day with my grandfather, I'd go hunting.

We'd wake up well before dawn. Dad and I would put on our hunting gear and sneak out the front door while it was still dark. We'd walk across the yard, shoes wet with dew, and knock on Grandpa's door. He would answer, and we'd pile into his old yellow Jeep.

We'd take the gravel road into the woods and spend the day hunting and laughing. We'd bag a few squirrels. Maybe even get a turkey or deer, depending on what's in season. In the late afternoon, we'd drive home to Grandpa's house and enjoy a meal together.

Then as the sun slipped under the horizon, we'd say goodbye for the last time. As I walk away, I'd glance over my shoulder for a final glimpse of my grandfather, thankful for one last day, thankful to have known him.

We take life for granted. We go about our days in a kind of fog, half paying attention to the people around us. We assume they will always be there. It usually takes a tragedy to wake us from our complacency.

Imagine you could spend one last day with someone who has passed. Whom would you choose? How would you spend it?

It's a moot point because you can't bring back someone who is gone. But it's a good exercise because it reminds us that we only have a limited amount of time with people. Therefore, we must learn to be fully present.

How can we do this? The answer is to give people gifts. There are three important ones.

THE GIFT OF TIME

For many years, my son Ben and I have enjoyed "Friday breakfast" before school. We started this when he was in junior high as a way to spend more time together.

The funny thing is that neither of us is a morning person, so we don't always say that much during breakfast. Sometimes there are long periods of silence as we eat.

But that is okay because the point is to be together, not necessarily to have a big, important conversation.

As a parent, I believe the cumulative effect of a thousand small conversations is much greater than a few big ones. It's the conversations about school, work, chores, relationships, technology, movies, future plans, and a hundred other things.

There is no such thing as "quality time." Time is time. Vacations, holidays, and birthdays are special events that create memories. But those pale in comparison to spending time with people you love in everyday life. Kids, as well as adults, spell L-O-V-E as T-I-M-E.

Time is the most precious resource you have. There is no better way to show you care about someone than investing it with them.

THE GIFT OF ATTENTION

Attention means giving someone your focus. Think back to your grade school days. When the teacher asked you to pay attention, they wanted you to focus your body and mind. It was all about eliminating distractions and listening to what the teacher had to say.

I have a hard time giving people my full attention. My mind is constantly racing with things I need to get done. I'm thinking about ideas for my writing or business. I'm reflecting on a client call that should have gone better. I'm wondering how to increase my podcast downloads or improve the marketing strategy of my next book.

When my son or wife comes into my office and wants to talk, they need my direct attention. The most loving thing I can do in that moment is turn away from my computer, look them in the eyes, and focus on them.

Attention is like a precious metal: everybody wants it, but nobody wants to give it. That's why it's so rare. We have a thousand things fighting for our attention. But we must remember that the people standing right in front of us are the most important thing in that moment.

THE GIFT OF ACCEPTANCE

Most of my painful memories as a kid involve P.E. class. I considered every moment of P.E. to be pure torture. But I could at least tolerate kickball since I had carefully worked out a system to stay invisible and avoid conflict at all costs.

When my team was on the field, my goal was to stay as far away from the ball as possible. Therefore, I always played the outfield and stood close to another kid, hoping they would be the one to handle the ball.

If the ball did happen to come my way, I didn't know where to throw it. I hated it when a runner was on base because that meant I would have to decide where to throw the ball. Somebody would inevitably be mad at me.

One day in the fifth grade, we went outside to play kickball. My team was on the field, and the other team kicked the ball way into left field. One of my teammates retrieved it and threw it to me.

I froze for a moment. There were too many things happening at once. I had no idea what to do, so I just randomly lobbed the ball toward the infield in an attempt to at least do *something*.

I'm sure there are P.E. teachers in the world who are empathetic to non-athletic kids, but ours was not one of them. He was a Type-A sports coach not known for his sense of subtlety. When I threw the ball, he looked square at me and shouted, "Why did you do that?" I had no answer. I just stood there looking stupid while all the kids gawked at me.

The incident lasted only a few seconds, and it happened nearly forty years ago. But I remember it like it was yesterday. That's how much we hate to be judged. We will do almost anything to avoid feeling stupid.

But the flip side of our dislike for judgment is that we love to feel accepted. When you make people feel loved and accepted, they will be a fan for life. Take the time to have meaningful conversations. Look people in the eye. Smile. Tell them what they mean to you. Send handwritten notes of appreciation.

Most people don't pay attention to these things. They take time and effort. That is why these principles are so valuable for building relationships.

Life is short. We only get so many trips around the sun. We have to make the most of the time we have. When you're with the people you love, be engaged. Be present. Give the gift of yourself.

9. FAITH

Embrace the Divine Mystery

"Never once in my life did I ask God for success or wisdom or
power or fame. I asked for wonder, and he gave it to me."
—ABRAHAM JOSHUA HESCHEL

This chapter is both the hardest and the easiest one
to write.

It is hard because I have not fully formed my thoughts
on this topic. I'm writing as a fellow traveler on the path
to knowledge and wisdom. But there is a book deadline,
so I press on.

At the same time, it is easy because I don't need to
have all the answers. Sometimes the best thing an author
can do is help you ask better questions.

The topic of faith is divisive. There are many reasons
for this. The most obvious one is that people have radically
different ideas about who God is, what He represents, or
if there even *is* a God to begin with.

Over the course of human history, many wars have been started and many people have died because of religious conflicts. That's why I tread carefully.

I started my faith journey as a young Christian in a small evangelical church in southern Missouri. I was taught to have a personal relationship with God, to have a daily quiet time where you search the Bible for God's guidance, and to attend church regularly.

Then as a Christian college student, and later as a pastor and seminary student, I was taught to interpret and teach the Bible to help people learn what God wanted from them. The evangelical world works on the assumption that we can clearly understand the Bible, and God can communicate directly with us. There is very little room for mystery.

As so often happens to people who have grown up in the church, I began to doubt what I had learned as I got older. For several years in my twenties, I went through a real crisis of faith. I have always been a student of science and astronomy. The more I learned, the more I started to seriously doubt if any of it was true: God, the Bible, my faith, the whole enchilada.

The problem was that I was a worship pastor at the time. It is hard not to feel like a complete fraud when you're leading people to worship a God you aren't even sure is there.

As I got into my thirties, this crisis of faith continued, but I went to great lengths to hide my doubt. By this time, I was teaching at a Christian college. Even though I was teaching Bible and ministry, I felt less pressure to conceal my doubts since I was no longer a pastor.

Ironically, it was a course in theology that brought my faith back around.

JEWISH, ORTHODOX, CATHOLIC

When I became a professor, one of my major responsibilities was revamping our music program for church worship leaders. We created a new course called "Theology and History of Worship," and I was assigned to teach it.

However, I didn't want to just lecture on the topic. I wanted to help students experience different expressions of their Christian faith firsthand.

As part of the course, I took the class to a Friday night Shabbat service at a local Jewish congregation. The people there were welcoming and kind. They took time to answer our questions and even fed us. I secretly wondered why many Christian people did not seem to be as welcoming as the people at the Jewish congregation.

We also visited a couple of Greek Orthodox churches in St. Louis. I had never visited an Orthodox church until I taught this course. The priests in both churches were welcoming and gracious. In both places, I was overwhelmed by a sense of mystery, art, and beauty. It also made me sad that for the most part, evangelical churches were only interested in the creative arts if it had something to do with music or video.

Then finally, we also visited the Cathedral Basilica in St. Louis. Commonly called the "new cathedral" even though it is over a hundred years old, the building is a stunning mixture of Greek and Roman styles. When you walk inside, you can't help but feel overwhelmed by the glittering mosaics and architecture.

I find it interesting that the Orthodox and Roman Catholic traditions construct and decorate their worship spaces to make you feel like you are one step closer to heaven. They emphasize God's transcendence, majesty, and grandeur.

On the other hand, people in the evangelical tradition try to make their worship spaces as warm and accessible as possible. They emphasize God's immanence, His nearness to us.

These experiences were good for both me and my students. I am an analytical person who always needs to understand systems and processes. I thought if I could just understand more about God, I would feel closer to Him. But my constant need for answers only left me with more questions.

My encounter with these different traditions had a surprising effect. My heart softened, and I began to let go of my need to have God figured out. This was a significant change in how I had grown up. When you are raised in the evangelical church, you are taught to be certain that God is there, the Bible is true, and that your understanding of Him is correct.

Even though I wasn't a hundred percent sure about any of those things, I felt free to embrace my faith anyway. I had a new awareness of my own intellectual limitations. It felt good. I was at peace.

CERTAINTY IS NEVER CERTAIN

One of the most valuable things I took away from seminary was reading a little book called *The Myth of Certainty* by

Daniel Taylor. Taylor argues that it's impossible to have certainty about your faith. The best we can do is look at the evidence and make a calculated decision to embrace faith even though we don't have complete certainty. He calls it "the risk of commitment." I like that.

The book helped me be okay with not knowing everything. In conjunction with being exposed to other faith traditions over the years, I have come to a place where I no longer need to understand everything.

I am inspired by the advances we have made in astronomy the last couple of decades. We are learning more and more about the universes (perhaps universes?) and the nature of reality. We have barely scratched the surface of our understanding.

But this knowledge does not crowd out a commitment to God. Instead, it should make us even more committed to the idea of a Designer or Architect who has put this all together.

As I look at the history, beauty, and the evidence for the historical integrity of the Bible, that is the faith system that seems to align best with reality as I understand it. In the evangelical tradition, there is a great emphasis on sharing the Gospel and helping introduce others to Jesus.

As a younger Christian, I went through many courses designed to help us explain and defend our faith.

I have come to the place in my life where I no longer feel the need to "defend" anything. I don't have any interest in being a religious zealot or a spiritual crusader. I never understood why so many Christians chose the metaphor of a "soldier" as the best way to represent God to the world.

It seems to me that the best evidence for the existence of God is a Christian who acts like Jesus. Jesus was joyful, humble, kind, and generous. He spent a lot of time with broken people and the outcasts of society.

Jesus had little regard for pointless religious traditions. He was more concerned with what was in a person's heart than the exterior image they were trying to project. I have always thought it was fascinating how Jesus reserved his harshest criticism for religious leaders.

Most days, I am pretty far from acting like Jesus. I have a stunning propensity for being selfish and judgmental. I have a big ego at times. I get cranky with my family. Most days, I don't feel like a very good Christian. But I'm trying.

Even if we somehow discovered that God doesn't exist, we can all agree that the way Jesus lived is a pretty good example for us all. He was, and is, the best of us.

WHAT DOES IT ALL MEAN?

So where does that leave us? If *faith* is a word we should live by, what does it mean on a day-to-day basis? I suggest two things.

First, it is important to let go of the need for certainty. Some personality types have an easier time with this than others. This was a struggle of mine for many years. But the sooner you can accept the idea that you will never have everything figured out, that you can never put all the puzzle pieces of knowledge together into one coherent whole, the more you will be at peace.

Life is like a roller coaster. You can enjoy the ride without needing to understand how all the machinery works.

Second, it is important to keep searching for wisdom. I know this sounds like the opposite of what I just said. But you don't need to be certain about everything to be wise. The wisest people can admit they don't know it all.

What is the point of wisdom and knowledge? Is it simply to be smarter or to win trivia games? The purpose is to help you live a more fulfilled and meaningful life. Wisdom should lead you to more humility, kindness, and maturity. God gives us wisdom in many ways, including our interactions with other people, our personal experiences, the Bible, prayer, and reading.

It is impossible to know everything. That is okay. Life is not about cramming our heads full of knowledge no matter what the academic world may say. Life is about the journey.

What happens when you embrace the mystery of life and commit to a God you don't fully understand? The journey becomes an adventure like no other.

10. ENCOURAGEMENT

Light Someone's Darkness

"No act of kindness, no matter how small, is ever wasted."

—AESOP

The year 1996 was a year full of highs and lows. I graduated from college, got married, and started my first full-time job. It was also the year my parents divorced after 26 years of marriage.

Having been around the block of life for 47 years now, and having been married, ironically, for 26 years myself, I am fully aware that people are human and that marriages end all the time. But I honestly never saw this one coming.

I still remember the call from my dad. I was working as a part-time pastor at a small church in Illinois on the weekends. One afternoon, I was in the church building and heard the phone ring in the kitchen. I picked up and was surprised to hear my dad's voice on the other end.

My first thought was, *Who died?* It was unusual for him to call the church. He said he and my mom had separated and that she had moved out. I don't remember any other details of the conversation because I had stopped listening. The news was such a shock that I couldn't process any other information.

I spent the next few days in a complete fog. I'm not sure how I made it through the sermon I preached the next morning. I still went to my college classes that week, but I was in emotional shock, walking around like some kind of zombie.

Many people showed small acts of kindness as I was going through this personal crisis. But one stands out in particular.

My classmate Joe Lieway was originally from Africa and had come to the U.S. to study the Bible at our college. His huge smile and even bigger personality made him larger than life. He radiated joy and laughter wherever he went.

A few days after I got the news, I went to my mailbox and found a small handwritten card from Joe. He affirmed that God's strength would help get me through that difficult time. He encouraged me to keep my head up.

The card probably cost fifty cents in our college bookstore. I'm sure it only took him a few moments to write. But I kept the card and have thought about it dozens of times over the years. To me, it is priceless.

Even better, Joe came to teach at our school a few years after I started working there. I had the privilege of receiving his joy and encouragement many times in the years we worked together.

What's going on here? What is encouragement, why do we need it so badly, and how does it work?

WHY ENCOURAGEMENT WORKS

I'm not usually a big fan of defining words because it sort of kills the fun. But in this case, I'll make an exception.

The word *encouragement* is made up of two words. First, you have the prefix *en* which means "to make or put in." Second, you have *courage* which refers to bravery, the quality someone must possess to face an obstacle, danger, or challenge. When you encourage someone, you are making them courageous or putting bravery inside them.

The opposite of *encourage* is *discourage*. A discouraged person has had their courage or bravery taken away by something or someone. Encouragement is the act of giving someone back their courage.

The corporate world thinks of encouragement a "soft skill" and would put it far down the list of qualities for a job candidate. When is the last time you saw "encourager" listed as a job skill on someone's resume?

Even so, it's one of the most important personal qualities you can ever develop. Most people try to hide their pain, fear, and discouragement. Earlier in the book, I referenced a quote attributed to Plato, but I'll repeat it here since it's so crucial: "Be kind, for everyone you meet is fighting a hard battle."

No matter what kind of happiness someone projects on the outside, there is always a little (or a lot) of fear on the inside. It's human nature. It doesn't mean everyone is driven by fear. It just means everybody needs a little encouragement.

Remember, people's number-one need is to feel loved, validated, and affirmed. When you fill someone's emotional bucket, they will remember it forever.

"But Kent," you ask, "if we all want encouragement so much, why do so few people practice it?" That's the million-dollar question, isn't it?

There is a pretty simple explanation: most people only think about themselves. It takes a mature, emotionally healthy person to be an encourager. That is why you must pay attention to other concepts in this book like gratitude, resilience, growth, and forgiveness. You must have something in your own emotional bucket if you want to help fill other people's buckets.

In addition, it also takes an attentive person to be an encourager. You must pay attention to people around you. If not, you will miss the signs that someone needs a kind word or a little help. You can be the nicest person in the world but still be self-absorbed.

If you want to be an encourager, you have to keep your chin up. You can't notice other people if you're always gazing at your navel.

THE MOST POWERFUL WAY TO ENCOURAGE OTHERS

There are many ways to help others be courageous. But I want to focus on one method that is simple yet powerful: sending handwritten cards in the mail.

When you go to the mailbox each day, which pieces do you open immediately? The ones that are handwritten. Everybody likes to receive something that was created just for them. This is why handwritten notes work so well.

Here are a few tips on making this as simple and effective as possible.

First, buy stationery in bulk and keep it by your desk. I like 3.5" x 5" cards because they are small and stand out in a stack of mail. I buy a few boxes at a time online. My stationery has a typewriter on the front, but you can use whatever kind of card represents your personality.

You also need stamps. I buy these in bulk, usually a roll of fifty stamps at a time. If you have to go to the post office every time you want to mail a card, you won't do it. Keep everything you need within arm's reach.

Next, write just two or three sentences expressing your appreciation or encouragement. Keep it short and sweet. I like small cards because you can only write a few sentences on them. If you buy larger cards, you will feel obligated to write a lot and will avoid it since it feels like too much work.

If you want to add a unique touch, include a little trinket of some kind. I purchase small skeleton keys in bulk and often tape one of these to the inside top of the card. I write something like, "P.S. Here's a little reminder of your incredible power to unlock other people's potential." I customize it according to the situation.

(Pro tip: if you send an item like a key inside a card, make sure it is oriented vertically so it passes through the automated mail sorters without the key mangling the card.)

I also keep people's mailing addresses in the contacts on my phone so I can access them easily. Anytime I send something in the mail, I store the address for future reference.

This all sounds so simple and maybe a bit trite. But you would be amazed at the number of people who have told me how much they love the key. Sometimes these comments come years after I have sent a card. When you send a unique little object that is invested with meaning and you tie it to the individual person's situation, they will remember it for a long time.

People realize it's a hassle to send a handwritten card and include a special little gift. For that reason, hardly anyone does it. But you must be the exception. You must be the one person in your circle who not only notices the people who need encouragement or affirmation. You must be the one who takes five minutes to send a card they will remember for years.

Everyone in your life is going through a darker time than you realize. They are thrashing around on the shoreline getting bashed by the storms of life. Take a few moments to be an emotional lighthouse so you can help them find their way.

II. SUCCESS

Redefine What It Means to Win

"Many of life's failures are people who did not realize how close they were to success when they gave up."

—THOMAS EDISON

One recent Monday, I had five calls scheduled. They went like this:

Call #1: A friend interviewed me for her podcast. She was intrigued by my ghostwriting business and asked lots of questions. I felt like a winner.

Call #2: I asked a mentor for some advice about various business issues. He is extremely successful and people see him as a leader in his industry. I was grateful for his guidance and wisdom. But when I compared myself to him, I felt like a loser.

Call #3: I had a coaching call with a client who is working on a book. She is doing great, and I gave her some helpful guidance. I felt like a winner.

Call #4: A friend of mine scheduled a call to talk about some business opportunities related to his writing. However, he was in a very bad mood that day and I was on the receiving end of all his frustrations. Although I knew I had not done anything wrong, I ended the call feeling like a loser.

Call #5: A copywriter friend of mine wanted to connect and see how we could help each other. The call was a blast, and I felt like a winner.

Do you see a pattern here? When something good happened, or when something stroked my ego, I felt like a winner. But if there was conflict or something threatened my fragile ego, I felt like a loser.

You'd think at my age I wouldn't let my self-esteem be subject to the whims of everyday life and the normal interactions of business. But no. Sometimes I let the silliest things determine whether I feel good about myself.

I bet you struggle with the same thing.

WHAT SUCCESS REALLY MEANS

There are two perspectives we can take about success. Let's use the Olympics as a way to illustrate.

The first view is the "I won a gold medal" perspective. This person only feels successful if they achieve more than others or they get the most recognition. Anything less is unworthy and represents a failure.

The second view is the "I made it to the Olympics" perspective. This person knows that participating in the Olympics is a huge deal even if you don't win a medal. Not just anyone can sign up for the Olympics. You need to be an athlete in peak condition just to make it to the games. You are part of an elite group of people who are better at their sport than almost anyone else in the world.

The famous broadcaster Earl Nightingale once said, "Success is the progressive realization of a worthy goal." Success doesn't happen all at once. It's a process.

I would argue that success is the process itself. Success is not so much a destination. It's the journey that takes you there. That means you are successful anytime you are working toward a worthy goal. That's why every Olympic athlete is a winner even if they don't win a gold medal.

Let's reframe the two instances of feeling like a loser that I mentioned earlier. What is my goal? It is to learn, grow, and build a great business.

By that definition, the call with my business mentor was a success. Even though he is far more "successful" than me, I learned a few great tips about improving my business.

In the same way, the call with my angry friend was a success as well. It didn't feel like it at the time, but over the next couple of weeks we cleared the air and built a stronger friendship. I learned about some issues he is struggling with and am looking forward to helping him work through them.

Do you see the pattern? Even though an event or conversation can feel bad in the moment, it's actually a success if it helps improve some aspect of the journey.

You can reframe almost every perceived "failure" as a success if you use it as a learning tool.

YOU MIGHT BE A SUCCESS IF . . .

The comedian Jeff Foxworthy is best known for his "You Might Be a Redneck" bit. He says, "You might be a redneck if . . ." and then says a funny line. He repeats the phrase a couple dozen times, each time with a different punchline.

The comedy bit is a fun way to help us see the signs that maybe we're not so sophisticated after all. In the same way, it's helpful to be aware of some signs to help you know if you have a success mindset. You might be a success if . . .

You learn from every situation, even if it feels bad in the moment.

You seek out mentors and coaches to help you improve.

You always try to add value to people.

You look for the good in everyone.

You spend as little time around negative people as possible.

You apologize and make things right when you are wrong.

You invest in your personal development through reading, conferences, retreats, courses, and more.

You try to help others become more successful by teaching and mentoring others.

You say yes to new and challenging opportunities before you feel ready.

You set goals for yourself and do a little every day to achieve them.

You are chasing your curiosity and know you don't have it all figured out.

These are just a few of the qualities of success you can use as a gauge for your development.

If you make progress, you are successful. It's not about winning the medal or getting recognition. It's all about being the absolute best you can be and taking as many people with you as you can.

12. GROWTH

Get Used to Being Uncomfortable

"The only person holding you back is you."
—TONY ROBBINS

On September 12, 1962, President John F. Kennedy stood before a crowd of 40,000 people at Rice University in Houston, Texas. He had come to Houston to tour the new Manned Spacecraft Center and build support for the country's new space program.

Kennedy had set a goal for the United States to land a man on the Moon by the end of the decade. You have probably heard the most famous part of his speech:

But why, some say, the Moon? Why choose this as our goal? And they may well ask, why climb the highest mountain? Why, 35 years ago, fly the Atlantic? Why does Rice play Texas?

We choose to go to the Moon. We choose to go to the Moon in this decade and do the other things, not because they are easy, but because they are hard, because that goal will serve to organize and measure the best of our energies and skills, because that challenge is one that we are willing to accept, one we are unwilling to postpone, and one we intend to win, and the others, too.

When is the last time you heard someone challenge you to make life harder instead of easier?

So much of our modern lives are focused on making things easy and convenient. With each passing year, our cars have more bells and whistles. Our phones and computers get faster. Our businesses become more automated.

But does ease and convenience make life better? Does it always lead to more excellence and kindness? Or can we make an argument that discomfort is a vital pathway to success?

I believe we can. No one in the history of humanity has achieved anything worthwhile because it was easy. I'm not here to tell your life should be miserable. Not at all. Instead, I want to challenge you to embrace the idea that effort and discipline are a crucial part of your success.

Not only are they necessary—they are desirable. When you put in the work and watch yourself grow, it is the most satisfying feeling in the world. If you want to change, you must grow.

Let's talk about one of the most important ways to do that.

ESSENTIAL TIPS FOR READING

The renowned motivational speaker Charlie "Tremendous" Jones famously said, "You will be the same person in five years as you are today except for the people you meet and the books you read."

This has been true in my own life. Most of the positive changes in my life have come about either because of someone's influence or because of something I have read.

Reading will change you. That's why it's uncomfortable. A provocative book is the most dangerous thing in the world. Why else would schools ban certain books?

If you're not reading, you're robbing yourself of fresh insights and creative ideas. In most cases, it takes an author years to write a great book. You can then read it in just a few hours. A book is another person's knowledge and wisdom in condensed form. There is no way to read a great book and stay the same.

That is why I have devoted my professional life to writing books! It's hard to think of a better use of my time and energy.

Here are a few essential tips for getting the most out of reading.

1. **Redeem some of the time you are already wasting.** If I'm not careful, I can waste twenty or thirty minutes watching a *Star Wars* analysis video or mindlessly scrolling through social media. We all have an entertainment drug of choice. We can use some of this time for reading.

2. **Use small pockets of free time.** You have lots of little chunks of open time on an average day. It might be fifteen minutes waiting at the doctor's office or ten minutes waiting to pick up your kid from school. These little blocks of time don't seem to matter in the moment, but they add up to several hours of reading time per week.

3. **Break up your reading into small chunks.** Let's say you're reading a 250-page book and want to finish it within a week. That's about 36 pages per day. If you break it up into two chunks of reading time per day, that's only 18 pages per session. Assuming a reading speed of one page per minute, that's less than 20 minutes, twice a day. It's even less time if you're reading a shorter book.

4. **Always have a book with you.** This is easy if you use an e-reader. I still prefer reading print books,

which is why I almost always have a print book with me. I've even been known to take a book to a St. Louis Cardinals baseball game. (Strunk & White's *The Elements of Style* is small enough to fit inside a jacket pocket. Just saying.)

4. **Listen to audiobooks.** The best thing about audiobooks is that you can listen while you do something else. I usually listen while I'm driving or doing dishes. You can also speed up the audio and get through a book faster.

If you use these suggestions to maximize your reading time, you will be amazed at your personal and professional growth. But it all starts with being intentional and putting in a little effort.

DON'T DESPISE THE CHISEL

Michelangelo was one of the greatest artists in history. It's hard enough to be a master of one skill. Yet he mastered three: sculpture, architecture, and painting.

He once remarked, "I saw the angel in the marble and carved until I set him free." He didn't *create* the angel of out the marble. He removed everything that didn't belong until the angel was revealed. It had been there all along.

What if the angel had resisted the chisel because it was too painful? Then it could have never been set free from the marble.

You and I are like angels waiting to be freed. Every time we go through a painful experience or choose growth over stagnation, the chisel of life removes a tiny piece that reveals the beauty and strength inside.

Does it often hurt? Yes? But is it necessary? Yes.

Don't despise the events and habits that can make you stronger. The goal of life is not to be comfortable. The goal is to reach your full potential and help others reach theirs, too.

We choose to grow. Not because it is easy, but because it is hard.

13. FREEDOM

Live on Your Own Terms

"Be yourself; everyone else is already taken."
—Oscar Wilde

Freedom. It's the quintessential American ideal. But what does it really mean?

Most people would say things like freedom to worship, freedom to travel, freedom to vote, or freedom to speak your mind. Freedom is woven into the very fabric of who we are as a people.

But freedom has a dark side as well. When you pursue freedom without discipline or purpose, it's easy to get yourself in trouble.

I know from firsthand experience. I talk about this in more detail elsewhere in the book, but I came to a place in my life where I was no longer happy with my direction. I was mostly ignoring my gifts and not leading our family well financially, either by saving or earning more.

The "freedom" I had to spend whatever I wanted through the use of credit cards turned out to be a horrible prison. It left us deeply in debt and I couldn't see any options. We could barely make ends meet. Our debt included a car loan, a mortgage, and several maxed out credit cards.

Between the two of us, Melanie and I brought home less than the median household income in America. Once I started doing freelance work in 2016, that increased by a few thousand dollars per year. But between the mortgage, credit cards, car loan, and living expenses, we had virtually nothing to put into savings at the end of each month. I knew that if I didn't do something soon, we were headed for a catastrophe.

FAILURE UPON FAILURE

I don't want to make it sound like life is all about money. It's not. Money doesn't magically make your life perfect. But it does solve a lot of problems in your life.

Another way of saying it is that money won't give you happiness, but a lack of money sure does cause a lot of grief.

The finance guru Dave Ramsey talks about the concept of a "bigger shovel" when earning money. This means doing work that is more highly valued and therefore pays more. It's hard to get out of debt and earn significantly more when you have a job teaching college and a side hustle bringing in a few thousand dollars per year.

I clearly needed a bigger shovel. But which one?

I tried several side hustles over the next few years. One summer, I borrowed a couple thousand dollars to buy into a network marketing business featuring health products. I completely failed within a few weeks.

Another summer, I spent all my free time selling books on Amazon. I wanted to reduce my extensive personal library but also make some money. So I listed, shrink-wrapped, labeled, and shipped about a thousand books to Amazon. I sold a couple hundred of these, but the rest of the inventory wasn't moving.

In a cruel irony, I ended up paying Amazon to destroy the rest of the books because it was cheaper than paying them to continue storing them. Another failure.

Then in 2019, I began trying anything that looked like a decent possibility just to see what would stick. I applied for several jobs related to writing or education, hoping one would pan out. One of the jobs required an extensive application process requiring a couple dozen hours of assessments. Over one thousand people applied, and I made it into the top fifty candidates.

I was so sure I was going to get the job that I started to research coworking spaces in the area. I mentally resigned from my job and even told a couple of my colleagues I would probably be leaving soon. But then I received the inevitable email telling me I wasn't selected.

Later that summer, I thought I'd try my hand at business consulting. I connected with a person in the dental industry who wanted me to develop a proposal involving writing, publishing, podcasting, and content development. I wanted this to succeed so badly that I stayed home to work on the proposal while my wife and son went on vacation with her family.

I spent about sixty hours researching and writing the proposal. I was sure she would love it and felt confident this was my big break. However, the proposal was rejected via text message within about twenty minutes of sending it.

At this point you might wonder, "Kent, why did you get distracted with all these other options? Why didn't you just focus on writing?" The answer is because I didn't know how to create a career based on writing. I didn't have enough confidence to feel it was a viable pathway.

I had never felt so discouraged in my life. The only thing that was working was freelance writing gigs, but those didn't pay much. Thus I stayed in my college job and started school that fall in a very bad mood.

Little did I know that things were about to change.

MAKING THE LIST

One September afternoon, it dawned on me that I had been approaching this completely backward. Instead of applying for jobs that I hoped would work out, what if I focused on the essential qualities I was looking for in a career, then custom-built it to match those criteria?

I grabbed a legal pad and began to write down all the things I wanted in my ideal job. I boiled it down to a list of five things:

1. **Freedom to work on my own schedule.** I was tired of someone else telling me where to be and how long I needed to stay there.

2. **Freedom to work from anywhere.** I was tired of fighting St. Louis traffic for an hour each day.

3. **Freedom to set my own income.** I was tired of working in a college job where my salary had nothing to do with how hard I worked or how well I performed. I wanted a business where the only limit to my compensation would be my own creativity and intelligence.

4. **Freedom to work with highly successful business leaders.** In order to earn more, I had to spend more time around people who could teach me how to be successful.

5. **Freedom to focus on writing, my main marketable skill.** I no longer wanted to teach courses or do other work that didn't excite me or contribute to what I was building.

As I thought about the different types of work that fit my criteria, I could only come up with two possibilities: copywriting and ghostwriting. I settled on ghostwriting because I had already written a couple of books and knew that world. There was also the "mystery" factor. People were always curious about ghostwriting, which I hoped would open some conversations. All in all, it seemed like the shortest route to success.

In addition, I had heard that an acquaintance of mine, Nick Pavlidis, was getting ready to launch a course called Ghostwriter School. He was a former attorney who had transitioned into a successful ghostwriting career. I asked Nick if I could be a guinea pig for the course, and he graciously agreed.

A few months after going through the course, I signed my first book client, then a second soon afterward. It has kept on building from there.

As a result of setting a clear vision for my business and then doing the work to build it, we were able to pay off a significant amount of debt, put money in savings for the first time, and begin making some home repairs.

DO YOU WANT A LIFE OF FREEDOM?

If you resonate with anything in this chapter, maybe it's time to make your own list of criteria. What is most important to you? What kind of life do you want to build?

Your list probably won't be the same as mine. That's okay. Your list should be unique to you. Start by envisioning the kind of life you want to live, then figure out how to fit work and career into it.

You will make mistakes on the road to freedom. The key to reducing your mistakes is getting clear on what kind of life you want, and what kind of work can get you there. Too many people build their life around their work when it should be the other way around.

The shortest pathway to a life of freedom is usually building your own business. It is the only way to totally control your own fate. Otherwise, you will always be at other people's mercy. You put yourself at risk if you abdicate decisions about income, employment, and your future to someone else. Nobody will care about your future as much as you do.

Don't leave your future to chance. Live on your own terms. Be free.

14. IDENTITY

Stop Waiting for Approval

"Figure out who you are and then do it on purpose."
—DOLLY PARTON

I was never one of the cool kids. Mind you, I was never an outcast or a social pariah. But my whole life, I have always felt like I was on the fringes, excluded from the inner circle for reasons I couldn't explain.

I was a band and choir geek in high school. I went to a small-town school with a few hundred students. Many of us were involved in the arts. I was certainly no slouch. But in spite of being in all the school plays and even winning the talent show one year, I was still never part of that elusive "in" crowd.

My high school was probably just like yours. There was a group of a dozen kids or so whom everyone admired. They determined who was in and out. Even the teachers seemed to like them more.

At our school, this group had all been friends since grade school. I never figured out how to get in or why it was so important to me. Even today, when I check social media and see conversations between these people, I admit that I feel a little twinge of rejection.

Isn't that silly? My thirty-year class reunion takes place this year. I've been out of high school nearly twice as long as it took me to get from birth to graduation. Yet there is a tiny part of me that still wants to be accepted and celebrated by that group.

THE SQUARE PEG SAGA

In many ways, the story of the first half of my life is a saga of a square peg trying to fit in a round hole. I've always been a bit of an oddball who was trying to gain the acceptance of a group of people I admired.

Earlier in the book, I mentioned that I went to a small Christian college and signed up as a preaching major. I didn't really enjoy preaching and wasn't particularly good at it. I was much more excited about music, but preaching was the most respected major at our school. Plus, I didn't want to disappoint the people at my home church who had encouraged me to pursue ministry.

So I trudged on through the program and made good grades. Fortunately, I got a job as a worship leader after college, which aligned well with my skills. For a while, I felt like I was right where I needed to be.

When I was 29, I went back to the same school to be a professor. I was tasked with revamping our music program. As part of my continuing education, I got involved with a group of music professors from sister schools. I went to the annual meeting a few times and even hosted it at our school once.

These were wonderful, gracious people. I wanted so badly to feel accepted by them. But I always felt like a second-rate music professor who didn't deserve a spot at the big kids' table.

There were a couple of reasons for this. One was that I did not have a music degree. While all the other professors taught music theory and choir, I only taught worship leading and ministry courses. We hired other adjunct teachers to cover the music courses. The other professors did not really think of me on their same level. And truthfully, I wasn't.

Our school was also much smaller than most of theirs. Each of their schools had dozens of students in their music programs (which seemed like a big number to me). But most years, I could count the number of our music majors on two hands (some years, just one hand).

After I had been teaching for ten years, our school and our music program began to falter. Enrollment was going down, and I didn't have the resources I needed for a competitive music program. I was almost 40 years old and had spent the majority of my life trying to please other people and gain their approval. But it wasn't working.

THE CONVERSATION THAT CHANGED EVERYTHING

One day around this time, I was standing in the kitchen talking to Melanie. She was cooking something on the stove as I was droning on about my latest book idea. We had been married almost twenty years, and she had heard countless book ideas in that time. The problem was that I never followed through on any of them. I had never written a book.

Something snapped within her. She turned toward me and gave me *the look*.

I said, "What's wrong?"

She gave an exasperated sigh. "Kent, I've heard you talk about writing a book for years. You're always talking about all these ideas, but you never follow through with anything. At this point, I'm tired of hearing about it because I've stopped believing you're ever going to do it."

I was shocked and a little hurt by her comment. But I knew she was right. Her reverse psychology worked and had the intended effect. I thought, *I'll show her!* and immediately started working on my first book, which eventually became a guide for church leaders on using the productivity app Evernote.

Only a few dozen people ever read that book, but the experience gave me the confidence to write the next one. It also led to starting a podcast, doing freelance writing, and eventually working as a full-time writer.

Melanie had been telling me for years to write. She knew it was my dream. But I was spending so much time seeking approval from people in the ministry and teaching fields—things I didn't even want to do anymore—that I was neglecting the very thing I should have been doing all along.

At heart, I'm a writer. That's who I was created to be. I spent a long time running away from that calling.

Now I can join my voice with the millions of other husbands since the dawn of time who have said, "I should have listened to my wife."

GIVE APPROVAL INSTEAD OF SEEKING IT

As I mentioned at the beginning of this chapter, I was never one of the cool kids . But today, at age 47, I'm finally cool with that.

When you know who you are and what you have to offer to the world, you realize that it's a waste of time to seek other people's approval. But you can also turn this concept on its head. Instead of seeking approval, be the one who gives it.

Be the man or woman who inspires, encourages, mentors, trains, and teaches others. Be the person who gives people a hand up in life. Be the leader who helps others be who they are, even if that means they need to leave your orbit and join someone else's.

Your destiny is not set in stone. You get to determine who you are and where you want to go. Don't try to wrestle your way into the cool kids' circle. Instead, create a new and better circle everyone else wants to join.

15. GRATITUDE

Appreciate What You've Been Given

"He is a wise man who does not grieve for the things which he has not, but rejoices for those which he has."
—EPICTETUS

As a high school kid, I was obsessed with playing Super Mario Bros. 3. Since my family didn't own an NES (Nintendo Entertainment System), I had to go to my girlfriend's house to play it. I would sit there for hours just trying to make it past World 3 (Water Land).

Super Mario Bros. 3 is a far more challenging game than the original Super Mario Bros., and also more fun. (I'm politely ignoring the substandard Super Mario Bros. 2.) My favorite part of the game was getting power-ups, which are items that give you unique powers.

Some of the best power-ups include: the Fire Flower, which lets Mario shoot fireballs; the Frog Suit, which lets Mario swim easier, and the Super Mushroom, which turns the original Small Mario into Super Mario and lets him take an extra hit before losing his life.

Wouldn't it be nice if there were real-life power-ups, special abilities that gave you extra insight, strength, or skills? Most people don't believe they exist.

Power-ups do exist, but not in the way you think. You're not going to walk down the street and spot a Fire Flower or Frog Suit, but there is one power-up that can give you a new perspective on life and radically improve your outlook. It's called gratitude.

Gratitude is a simple concept that we take for granted. It may not seem as exciting as other personal qualities like vision or creativity. Yet gratitude is much more subtle and equally as powerful, especially when you consider all the people who have helped you over the years.

As an American, independence is baked into my DNA. We believe it is essential to be "self-made." We are not geared to think about ourselves as part of a larger community the way other cultures around the world do.

Independence can be a great strength, but it's also a liability. As the poet John Donne wrote, "No man is an island." Nobody accomplishes anything worthwhile on their own. There are always others who have supported you and given you the resources you need.

ONE AUTHOR, HUNDREDS OF HELPERS

Here's an example. My second book was a short volume called *The Artist's Suitcase: 26 Essentials for the Creative Journey*. Even though I am the author, it took a whole team of people to bring the book to life. The editor, cover designer, beta readers, and launch team all played a role, not to mention my email subscribers, friends, and social media contacts who helped make the book a success.

And then there are people who have encouraged me as a writer, such as my wife Melanie, my junior English teacher, Mrs. Mathis, and my mom, Mary McEntire.

That's just the tip of the iceberg. What about people like Jeff Goins, Michael Hyatt, Honorée Corder, Dan Miller, and Joanna Penn? Those are all authors and business leaders who helped give me the courage and confidence to write a book.

The only author listed on that book cover was me, but lots of other people helped bring it to life.

You see, behind every person who accomplishes something worthwhile, there are dozens, if not hundreds, of others who have helped them. The same is true for you. No matter who you are or what you have achieved, you have not done it by yourself. Think about all the friends, family members, coworkers, authors, teachers, and others who have contributed in large and small ways to your success .

When you think about this, you begin to appreciate what you have and the people who have helped you. The word "appreciate" means to "increase in value." If you buy a house or another asset that goes up in value, it appreciates. And when you appreciate those who have helped you, your relationship goes up in value, too.

You can understand gratitude on an intellectual level, but in order to release its power, you must express it. Let's talk about some specific ways to do this.

THREE WAYS TO EXPRESS GRATITUDE

The first way to express gratitude is privately. One of the most effective ways to do this is by keeping a "gratitude journal." I have a small paper journal I use just for this, but a digital journal or computer file works just as well.

There are only three things I write on the page: the date, "Today I am thankful for …," and then three things

I'm thankful for that day.

For example, here are some of the items I've written in my gratitude journal over the last few months:

Today I am thankful for …

- *Nice weather that isn't too hot.*

- *The opportunity to choose my attitude and actions each day.*

- *A wife who is supportive of my personal and professional goals.*

- *Signing a new book client this month.*

- *Ben – a great kid who is funny, kindhearted, and caring.*

- *I feel like the darkness has lifted a little bit—got a good night's sleep. Been dealing with a little bit of depression the last few days.*

- *My back feeling better after hurting it on a hike a few weeks ago.*

- *Getting a good start on my new book yesterday.*

I limit myself to three items every day to keep it short and sweet. Sometimes I write in the morning, sometimes in the evening. Sometimes I forget about doing it altogether. But I try to do it daily. The whole process literally takes less than two minutes.

The second way to express gratitude is personally. A personalized, handwritten note is extraordinarily powerful. I talk elsewhere in the book about my system for doing this, so I won't belabor it here. One of my business mentors, Honorée Corder, sends a thank-you note in the mail every day. As a person who has received several of these the last couple of years, I can tell you that it makes you feel like a million bucks to receive one of these.

Finally, you can also express gratitude publicly. You can do this anytime you address a group of people, but the simplest way is by using social media. Whenever you want to recognize someone for how they have helped you, tell a story about it.

Whenever I transitioned away from my college job into my business full-time, I wrote a long post on Facebook thanking the most important people who helped me along the way. I thanked St. Louis Christian College, where I worked for many years. I thanked Vincent Pugliese and Nick Pavlidis, two business leaders who had an immense impact on my business mindset. I thanked my clients, who make my business possible.

And of course, most of all, I thanked my amazing wife Melanie and our incredible son Ben. It absolutely wouldn't have happened without their support.

When you practice gratitude every day, it really does affect your attitude. You become more positive, and you begin to notice the little ways people help you. You stop taking things for granted. Most importantly, you become a more positive influence on people.

Ironically, I've never been able to beat Super Mario Bros. 3 even though I've been playing it for over 30 years. But that's okay. Video games are pretty far down the list of priorities compared to practicing gratitude.

Why? Because gratitude is the ultimate power-up.

16. RESILIENCE

Bounce Back Stronger

"Character consists of what you do on the
third and fourth tries."
—JAMES MICHENER

In every good movie, there is an "all is lost" moment. That is the screenwriter's term for the moment when all hope is gone and everything looks darkest for the hero.

In *The Wizard of Oz*, the moment comes when Dorothy and her friends are trapped by the Wicked Witch of the West in one of her castle turrets. Her guards have them surrounded as the Wicked Witch sets the Scarecrow on fire.

In *Raiders of the Lost Ark*, the moment comes when Indy and Marion are tied to a stake. The Nazis are about to open the Ark of the Covenant, believing they will now have the ultimate weapon.

In *The Empire Strikes Back*, the moment comes when Darth Vader slices off Luke's right hand and announces the shocking news that he is Luke's father. All Luke can do is contort his face into the most dramatic "Nooooo!" you've ever seen on screen.

The stories are different, but they have one thing in common. The heroes didn't just sit passively by and accept their fate.

Dorothy picked up a bucket of water to put out the flaming Scarecrow but accidentally melted the Wicked Witch. Indy and Marion shut their eyes so the Angel of Death wouldn't destroy them. Luke took his chances falling down an air ventilator shaft rather than join Darth Vader.

What's true in movies is true in life. There comes a moment when all hope is lost and you have to make a decision. Are you just going to lie down and die? Or will you gather your strength and do something about it?

Resilience is the name for this ability to rise up in the face of overwhelming odds. Maybe it's not so much of an ability as it is a primal desire to fight, to stand against certain doom, to rise up like a reborn phoenix from the ashes and keep going.

Resilience isn't a quality only for the strong or the brave. It's the quality that makes you brave even when everything is going wrong. Everyone has a train wreck every once in a while. The question is not whether you will have one, but what you will do when you have one.

That's a question I faced one cold December day in 2019, as I sat on the floor of my home office wondering how I was going to crawl my way out of a huge mess.

17 CENTS IN THE BANK

Melanie and I both grew up in homes where we celebrated Christmas. When we got married and eventually had Ben, it was important to continue the traditions we loved. We never went crazy with Christmas gifts, but neither did we go cheap. We usually spent a few hundred dollars total on gifts—far less than the average American family.

Even so, it always stretched us financially come Christmas each year. I never earned much as a Christian college professor, and neither did Melanie as an events manager at a local art center. That's why I had been doing freelance writing jobs the previous couple of years. One particular client paid me a few hundred dollars every four months to write content for his website. I was always excited when that payment would come because it meant a little extra cushion for our family.

As 2019 drew to a close, I expected another payment from this client by the middle of the month. I planned on using the money to cover Christmas. It would be just enough. Perfect!

In early December, we started buying gifts with our regular money, expecting that client payment to come through in the middle of the month. That way, we could cover groceries and other bills the second half of the month. I was a little nervous because there was always the possibility the payment wouldn't come through for some reason.

Sure enough, about the middle of the month, I received the news that the client was taking a break for a few weeks. This meant the payment wouldn't be coming until sometime in January. We were in trouble.

Christmas came and went as usual, except that my stomach was filled with a huge knot, wondering how we were going to survive the next week or two until each of us got paid or the client money came through. The day after Christmas, I logged on to our bank account. We had a grand total of 17 cents in checking, with no savings.

I had no idea how we were going to pay for groceries. I started looking around my home office for things to sell on

Craigslist or Facebook Marketplace. The best I could come up with was a few of my prized Blu-ray box sets, including the complete *Twilight Zone* collection and the extended editions of *The Lord of the Rings* movies. As I recall, I sold both of those for a total of twenty or thirty dollars.

I will never forget that "all is lost" moment, sitting cross-legged on my office floor surrounded by stuff I thought I could sell for a few dollars. The knot in my stomach was unbearable.

At that moment, I made a vow to myself: *I will never, ever let this happen again.*

I stayed true to my word. It has never happened since. Although I was grateful to have those lower-paying freelance writing gigs, I determined right then and there to do everything I could to build my business in addition to other streams of income.

We were in that situation mostly because of my poor budgeting. We could have avoided it altogether if I had been smarter and more disciplined with money.

Over the next year and a half, I worked hard to build our income. I was able to put enough in savings that I could transition fully into my business. It was an immense amount of work, and I got discouraged plenty of times.

It's hard to build a successful business as a side hustle. But I never once thought of quitting because I remembered the shame of having only 17 cents in the bank.

WHATEVER IT TAKES

In that "all is lost" moment, though, sitting there on my office floor in December 2019, I needed a short-term solution for cash. In addition to selling a few items, I found another source of cash.

A couple of days after Christmas, we visited my dad in Illinois. As we were opening up Christmas gifts, I noticed that my son Ben had received over $100 in cash from relatives. Melanie and I had received a couple of Amazon gift cards. We did a swap so Ben could have the Amazon cards, and we would have the cash. We needed the cash, and Ben loved to order things from Amazon. Everybody was happy.

Well, that's not entirely true. I was happy that we had a little cash to use for groceries. But I also felt ashamed that I had put us into such a bad situation that we had to use my kid's Christmas cash to get us through the next couple of weeks.

In hindsight, I should have borrowed a little money from my dad. He would have been happy to help. But I was too proud to ask.

It's hard to see your options when your back is against the wall. Even Dorothy had this problem. At the end of *The Wizard of Oz*, she discovered that she had the power to go home any time she wanted. But she never realized it.

When you are staring an overwhelming problem in the face, it's hard to feel strong, capable, resilient. But you can do it. It's time to push through the pain and do what you need to do.

It will probably not feel pleasant. It might be downright painful. But you have to climb the mountain if you want to see the view.

17. INTEGRITY

Do the Right Thing

"The supreme quality for leadership is unquestionably integrity. Without it, no real success is possible, no matter whether it is on a section gang, a football field, in an army, or in an office."
—Dwight D. Eisenhower

I n the first chapter of this book, I shared why we must take responsibility for our lives. But what happens when we refuse to take responsibility and try to pin the blame on someone else? We start "passing the buck."

The term "pass the buck" comes from the world of poker. On the frontier, players would use a small object such as a knife with a buckhorn handle to indicate whose turn it was to deal the cards. If the player did not want to deal, they would "pass the buck," thereby giving responsibility to the next person.

President Harry S. Truman famously kept a small sign on his desk that read, "The buck stops here." He wanted everyone to know that he accepted full responsibility for his decisions.

Truman is the rare exception. People have been passing the buck and avoiding responsibility since long before poker was invented. The first few chapters of Genesis tell the story of the first passing of the buck when Adam blamed Eve for giving him the forbidden fruit.

Whether it's men and women of the Bible, world leaders over the millennia, or the people in your everyday life, we humans will do almost anything to hide our mistakes rather than confess them.

I have faced this choice countless times over the years. Sometimes it has involved a big mistake, and sometimes it was something small. Or at least, something I *perceived* it to be small.

THE CASE OF THE MELTED RUG

Years ago, when we lived in northern Illinois, I spent a few days with my brother Don and his family. One morning after everyone had left, and I was at the house alone. I needed to iron a shirt but didn't want to drag out the ironing board. So I decided to iron the shirt on the living room rug instead.

After I finished, I set the iron aside and picked up my shirt to examine my handiwork. Beautiful! Then I looked down. To my horror, I discovered that I had melted part of the rug.

Rather than admitting what I had done, I rearranged the furniture slightly and slid a recliner over the melted part of the rug. Surely they wouldn't notice, right?

But my sister-in-law Stephanie uncovered my little scheme a short time later when she stepped on the melted part of the rug under the recliner. I was busted!

A few months later, they bought a new living room rug. Stephanie cut out the melted portion of the rug that was shaped like an iron, framed it, and gave it to me the following Christmas as a joke. To add to the fun, she attached a slip of paper with a few words from Numbers 32:23. It read, "YOUR SIN WILL FIND YOU OUT."

If I would have just admitted my mistake as soon as it happened, I would have saved a lot of embarrassment. Not to mention decades of ribbing from my family!

I keep the melted rug remnant in a box in my basement. Every time I come across it, I remember that it's easier to just confess.

I did the wrong thing hoping no one would notice. But there have been other times I have acted with integrity even though no one would probably ever notice.

NO ONE WOULD EVER KNOW

In addition to being a professor, I served in various other roles at our college. In 2012, our administrators asked if I would create some promotional videos. I said I would love to help, but it would require a substantial amount of time that semester.

The college could not pay me to do it, so I made a proposal. If they purchased a new MacBook computer for me to use for editing, I would do it for free. It would be a huge challenge to create high-quality video without a decent computer. I had been using an old PC laptop that would not get the job done.

The school agreed, and the President found a donor to cover the cost of the computer. I completed the video project and continued to use the MacBook until early 2021. (I was impressed I got nine years out of it.)

By that time, I was getting ready to leave my position at the college to work in my business full-time. I had also just bought a new MacBook with my own money but wanted to keep the old one as a backup.

Technically, the school still "owned" the old laptop. By that point, it was only worth a couple hundred dollars anyway. I had also personally paid for a new hard drive and upgraded RAM. I could make an argument that since I had paid for those items, the computer more or less belonged to me.

In addition, our administrative team had completely turned over since the school bought the computer. If I just kept the computer when I left the job, it wouldn't occur to anyone to even ask about it, much less question my decision to keep it.

Plus, I knew that our tech office would have no use for the computer. It would just sit on a shelf and gather dust.

Nevertheless, I felt compelled to officially purchase the old MacBook from the college. I explained the situation to our CFO, we agreed on $250 for the used computer, and I wrote out a check.

I probably could have justified keeping the computer. But in the end, I didn't want anyone to ever question it. It was much easier to do the right thing.

ARE YOU INTEGRATED OR FRACTURED?

I'm sure you relate to the stories I've just shared. Just like me, there have been times you have acted with integrity. And just like me, there have been times you have gone to great lengths to cover up your sins.

The word *integrity* is related to the mathematical term *integer*, which means a "whole number." It is also related to the word *integrated*. An integrated person is whole. What they appear to be is what they actually are. Each part of their life is integrated into the others. Talk to any person in their circle, and they will give you the same picture of this individual.

Contrast this with a *fractured* person, one who does not have integrity. They are not integrated. They live in the land of fractions, where everyone sees a slightly different piece of them. They spend a lot of energy keeping up appearances and trying to prevent people from finding out who they really are.

When I melted my sister-in-law's living room rug, how much emotional energy do you think I spent worrying whether she would find out? *A lot.* It was a relief when she found out because I no longer had to worry about being deceptive.

It's hard to be a person of integrity an *integrated* person—when you spend so much energy trying to hide the truth.

There are a lot of good reasons to practice integrity in the big and small things. For one, there is always the chance that you will get caught. It is best to go through life operating on the assumption that someone can see what you are doing at every moment.

Another way to look at this is to always ask yourself, "What would my mom think about this if she knew what I was doing?" That is a quick way to make you clean up your act!

But there is another, deeper reason to do the right thing: you will have a clean conscience. It is helpful to be motivated by the fear of getting caught, but external motivation can only go so far. The best motivation comes from inside your heart, from wanting to do the right thing because it aligns with who you are as a person.

But when you do the wrong thing—which you inevitably will, as we all do—make it right as soon as possible. Confess. Pay the fine. Say you're sorry. Replace the item you broke. Go above and beyond, and do more than is required.

When you do, you won't have to worry about people from different parts of your life talking to each other and getting different stories. You also won't have to worry about getting called out for a hidden wrong or those debts you still have to pay.

Come to think of it, I never did offer to pay for that rug. It seems I have a phone call to make.

18. FORGIVENESS

Let Go of the Baggage

"Darkness cannot drive out darkness; only light can do that. Hate
cannot drive out hate; only love can do that."
—MARTIN LUTHER KING, JR.

Imagine you are walking down the street with a large
suitcase. It is worn and tattered, nearly falling apart.
The seams have almost given way, and the wheels have
long since broken off, so you carry it by the handle.

With suitcase in hand, you trudge back and forth
on the same street, day after day. Some days you can
almost manage. You are nearly used to the weight and
inconvenience by now. But today you are so exhausted
you can barely move. You inch your way forward carrying
the same suitcase.

You hear someone walking behind you. A man passes
you, then gives you a strange look. Then he stops and
turns around.

"What have you got there?"

"This is my suitcase," you reply. "I carry it with me every day. Wherever I go, the suitcase goes."

"The suitcase must be very important to you."

"Oh yes, it's not just important. I've been carrying this suitcase for so long it's practically a part of me." You pause for a moment. "You might even say it's part of my identity."

Finally, the man gathers up the courage to ask the question you know is coming next. "So . . . what's in the suitcase, anyway?"

"Well, it's kind of personal. But I guess there's no harm in showing you."

The man approaches as you lay the suitcase flat on the sidewalk. "Give me a moment. I have to work the combination lock to open it," you say. "Nobody gets in this thing but me." The lock snaps open, and you push in the rusty clasps on either side.

As you open the suitcase lid, a confused look spreads across the man's face. "I don't understand," he says. "You're carrying a suitcase full of old bricks?"

"Oh, these aren't just any old bricks," you explain. "These are all my grudges. I have to carry them around so I never forget all the ways people have hurt me."

You take a dusty brick from the scattered pile in the suitcase and hand it to the man. "See, they're all engraved so I never lose track of them."

The man looks at it for a moment, then stoops down to examine the rest.

You continue, "Each one is etched with the person's name, date, and what they did to hurt me."

After a few moments, the man stops and looks at you with a sad gaze. "These bricks are so heavy. I don't know how you manage to carry all of them around."

With tears in your eyes, you confess, "I know it's killing me. But I just can't let them go."

WHY IS THIS SO DIFFICULT?

Everyone can see themselves in this story. We can all relate to the person who drags a suitcase around full of hurts and offenses. We all carry grudges. We remember who hurt us and why they were wrong.

And if we're honest, we have to admit there is a part of us that *enjoys* being hurt. We like the feeling that someone owes us something, even if we know that anger harms us.

Why do we do this? Why is it so hard to let go of grudges and offenses? Why do we stay angry?

Anger is our response to unmet expectations. Traffic is slow when we expected it to be faster, so we get angry. Our spouse didn't take care of the housework like we expected, so we get angry. Going to the DMV is a hassle and we expected it to be simple, so we get angry.

We have unrealistic expectations of people, systems, and life. But that doesn't completely explain anger.

Anger is also stored-up revenge. We hold on to anger, hoping we will get to use it against the other person at some point. How many times have you been in an argument with someone and you bring up something they did years ago? A tiny part of you held on to that offense so you could bring it back out at just the right time.

How does it feel? Does it get rid of the anger? No. It just makes it worse.

Knowing all this, why aren't we quick to forgive? Because letting go of the hurt and pain makes us vulnerable. We love to fight and argue. We like to hold on to our weapons. It's a way to protect our emotional territory.

But when we can learn to let go, that is where we find joy and peace.

GIVING & SEEKING FORGIVENESS

I know that issues of forgiveness, anger, and resentment can run deep within a person's psychology. I'm not a psychoanalyst or relationship expert, but I do have one piece of wisdom to offer about forgiveness: be quick to give it and quick to ask for it.

Every situation is different. Some hurts run extremely deep. But I do know one thing. The longer you hold on to anger, the more you will hurt yourself. As Yoda said in *The Empire Strikes Back*, "Fear leads to anger. Anger leads to hate. Hate leads to suffering."

Whenever you hold on to hatred, who do you think suffers most? It's not the person you hate. It's you and the people you love.

I'm not here to tell you *how* to forgive. Every situation is different. Some people offer forgiveness directly to the person who wronged them. Some people write a letter, especially if the person they are forgiving is dead. Everyone has their own pathway. But the important thing is that you find a way to let the anger go.

Likewise, when you've wronged someone, you must seek forgiveness. Do it quickly in the best way the situation merits. Depending on what you've done, there might be legal or financial consequences. In some cases, it's best not to communicate with the person you've wronged. But in most cases, especially in one-on-one relationships, you can ask them directly.

I wish I had understood this in the early years of our marriage. Melanie and I would get into an argument about something. Then because of my pride and my tendency to avoid conflict, we would have two or three days where we barely spoke to one another.

One of us would eventually apologize. Most of the time, it needed to be me since I was too proud to admit I was the biggest part of the problem.

Now that we have been married for 26 years, I couldn't tell you the last time we went to bed angry with one another. We try to live by a simple rule in our family. We all say, "I love you" to each other every night before bed. And we try to never go to bed angry.

It's not complicated. When you're wrong, say you're sorry, and do it quickly.

THE HARDEST PERSON TO FORGIVE

It's one thing to give forgiveness to someone who's hurt you, or seek forgiveness from someone you've wronged.

But the hardest person of all to forgive? Yourself.

The anger and frustration we harbor toward others is nothing compared to the self-hatred many people carry. Are you one of those? We all are at times. But if you struggle with forgiving yourself, if you wrestle with self-hatred, I want to tell you something.

You are wonderful.

You are worthy.

You are valuable.

You are strong.

You are amazing.

Maybe you're like the person in the story who carries around a suitcase full of bricks. But what if we add a twist to the story? When the stranger opens your suitcase, they can't find any other names on the bricks.

Why? Because they all have *your* name on them. The only person you can't forgive is yourself.

We have all sinned. We have all fallen short. Maybe you have done some *really* bad things. You can't let go of the guilt because it's too great.

I look at it this way: if God can forgive me, I can forgive myself, too.

You've been carrying around that suitcase far too long. It's time to leave it behind.

EPILOGUE

What We Leave Behind

A couple of years ago, I took a trip with my father and my son Ben to visit some of our older relatives. We made several stops and spent the whole day getting reacquainted with people we had not seen in a long time. Some of them were people my son had never met.

However, none of these relatives spoke a word. Our visits with them consisted of complete silence.

Why? Because they were all in the graveyard.

This may seem like a pretty morose trip, especially for a teenager. But young people need to have a direct connection with their ancestors. Like all of us, they need to come to grips with a basic fact of life.

We're all going to end up in the graveyard.

This doesn't have to be a depressing thought. It's actually quite liberating. When you accept that your life has an expiration date, you live differently. You realize that all the things we get so worked up about—the petty arguments, trivial pursuits, and small inconveniences of life—don't matter so much.

Most of all, this perspective makes us realize we have a limited amount of time to make a difference, to consider what we are going to leave behind for others.

Which begs the question . . . what *do* we leave behind for others, anyway?

THE IMPRESSION YOU LEAVE

Every human being carries a unique set of identifiers on their fingertips. No two fingerprints are alike. That is why fingerprints have long been used by law enforcement to identify suspects who have been present at a crime scene.

We leave fingerprints everywhere. We can't help it. Every time we touch something, we leave a print, a tiny yet unmistakable part of ourselves that changes the essence of the thing we have touched.

Fingerprints aren't just physical. They're emotional, too. Every time you interact with someone, you leave an emotional residue that goes straight to their core.

I like to call these "soulprints."

The soulprint you leave on others can build them up. Your words actions can help them rise to new heights.

You can make them better because of what you say or do.

Your soulprint can also tear others down. You can destroy another person with criticism, gossip, slander, and lies. These negative prints can emotionally cripple someone for the rest of their life.

Do you remember that time when another kid said something mean to you at school? Of course you do. All these years later, you remember it like it was yesterday. We never forget those scars.

For good or bad, it doesn't take much to leave a soulprint that changes someone's life.

A SOULPRINT CONVERSATION

A few years ago, I was trying to figure out my next career step. I had been a professor for over a decade and wanted to make a transition. Ideally, I wanted to build a business for myself, but I had no idea what that might look like.

The one thing I knew was that I needed to get around the right type of people who could give me guidance and opportunities.

I got involved in an online community led by the author and entrepreneur Dan Miller. (This was an early version of his 48 Days Eagles community, which continues to impact thousands of lives). I joined a podcasting group within this community and struck up a friendship with a producer named Rye Taylor.

Rye discovered I was a writer. One day he sent me a message asking if I would be interested in writing podcast show notes for one of his clients.

I happily accepted the freelance work. It turned into a collaboration that lasted several years. That opportunity opened many other doors as I met more people and built my confidence. Eventually I was able to transition into full-time writing.

It all started with that one invitation from my friend Rye. His words left a soulprint that changed the course of my life.

YOU HAVE THE POWER

Imagine if you asked the people in your life what kind of soulprint you've left on them. How would they respond?

Would they say you were kind? Generous? Thoughtful? That you made them a better person? That their life was better for having known you?

Or would they wince as they told you about that time you criticized them and crushed their confidence? Or how you focused on yourself and your own success instead of helping them when they really needed it? Would they say you were arrogant? Mean-spirited? That you mostly brought them pain and suffering?

Every day, we leave soulprints behind. Every word, every tone of voice, every social media post, every conversation, every engagement with a client or customer, every morsel of gossip you decide what to do with . . . they all leave a lasting impression.

Those impressions aren't just short-term. They can change someone's life trajectory and impact generations. You have enormous power to impact people with your words and actions.

Make no mistake. You *will* leave a soulprint on everyone you meet. The only question is, what kind of soulprint will it be?

When all is said and done, what will you leave behind?

ACKNOWLEDGMENTS

It's quite normal when you're working on a book project to gather help from a group of early readers as well as a book launch team. It's also typical to announce the book months ahead of its release to help ramp up the marketing and let people know when it will be available.

I chose not to use any of those since I wanted this book to be a surprise for my son Ben's 18th birthday. Nevertheless, several people helped bring this book to life in different ways.

Thanks to Kristi Griffith for the beautiful cover design and interior layout. You are a wonderful creative collaborator, and I'm so grateful for your patience and design skill. Thanks to Jennifer Harshman for the skillful editing which elevated every page of this book.

Thanks to my father, Don Sanders, and my mother, Mary McEntire, for instilling in me so many of the lessons in this book. I am blessed to have parents like you.

Thanks to my amazing wife, Melanie, for reading a draft of the book and offering tremendous feedback. Your insights were invaluable. Can you believe Ben is eighteen? It's been a wild ride, and there's no one I'd rather have as my companion. I love you.

And finally, thanks to my son Ben for being yourself. I love our talks, Friday breakfasts, and QT runs. Every parent should be so blessed to have a kid like you.

DISCUSSION GUIDE

I hope you've enjoyed reading *18 Words to Live By*. Even more, I hope you will test drive these principles in your own life. To that end, I've created a guide you can use for journaling, group discussion, or writing prompts. I hope these questions encourage you to reflect on what is important in life and how to keep it front and center.

I. Responsibility: Take Charge of Your Life

1. Are you willing to take responsibility for your own success? Be honest.

2. When is the last time you admitted a mistake or apologized to someone? What happened as a result?

3. If you feel frustrated by the state of your life right now, what is one thing you can do today to move in the right direction?

2. Courage: Act in the Face of Fear

1. What are you most afraid of right now?

2. When is the last time you acted with real courage? What did it feel like?

3. Who is the most fearless person you know? What makes them that way?

3. Empathy: See the World Through Another's Eyes

1. Do you find it hard to empathize with people? Why or why not?

2. Would your friends describe you as a good listener?

3. Describe the last person who made you feel really valued. What did they do to make you feel that way?

4. Generosity: Give From the Overflow

1. Do you have an abundance or a poverty mindset?

2. When is the last time someone did something generous for you? How did you respond?

3. Review the ten ways to be generous. How many of these could you put into practice within the next week?

5. Creativity: Partner with Great Collaborators

1. Have you ever worked with a creative partner? What was your experience?

2. Do you believe independence is overrated? Why or why not?

3. Is there someone you know who might make a great creative partner? Why not ask them to collaborate on a project?

6. Authenticity: Get Comfortable in Your Own Skin

1. What is a big mistake you have made? How can that experience help other people avoid the same thing?

2. What is the hardest thing about accepting yourself as you are?

3. Do you think George Bailey was a successful person? Why or why not?

7. Discretion: Watch Your Words

1. Think of conversations you've had in the last 48 hours. How could you have applied Robert Greene's principle, "Always say less than necessary?"

2. Do you think it is wise to have no opinion about most things? Why or why not?

3. When is the last time someone meddled in an argument you had with someone? How did it make you feel?

8. Presence: Wherever You Are, Be There

1. Which of the three gifts in this chapter is the hardest for you to give—time, attention, or acceptance? Which is the easiest?

2. If you could spend one more day with a loved one who has passed away, whom would you choose?

3. Think about someone in your life who needs encouragement. Which of the three gifts could you give them in the next 24 hours to brighten their day?

9. Faith: Embrace the Divine Mystery

1. Do you embrace the idea that God exists? Why or why not? What evidence would you give for either point of view?

2. Are you comfortable with the idea that you can never be totally certain about faith, that it involves the "risk of commitment"?

3. What are the ways you most enjoy learning?

10. Encouragement: Light Someone's Darkness

1. When is the last time you received a handwritten card in the mail? How did it make you feel?

2. Why do you think it is so hard for most people to pay attention to the emotional needs of others?

3. Think of one person in your life who needs encouragement. Are you willing to get the supplies and take a few moments to send them a note of encouragement?

II. Success: Redefine What It Means to Win

1. Do you agree with Earl Nightingale's definition of success as the "progressive realization of a worthy goal?" Why or why not?

2. Do you tend to be the "I won a gold medal" type of person or a "I participated in the Olympics" type of person?

3. Review the list of items in the "You might be successful if ..." list. Which ones describe you? Which ones do you aspire to?

12. Growth: Get Used to Being Uncomfortable

1. What tough situation are you going through right now that is helping you grow?

1. Review the suggestions for reading. Which of these can you put into practice today?

2. Do you see yourself as an angel in the marble, waiting for your potential to be released?

13. Freedom: Live on Your Own Terms

1. Do you want a life of freedom?
    Why or why not?

2. Have you ever considered starting your own business? What is appealing or intimidating about it?

3. Review the list of five criteria for freedom in this chapter. If you were to make your own list, what would be on it?

14. Identity: Stop Waiting for Approval

1. Have you ever tried to be one of the "cool kids"? Why made you want to be part of that group?

2. What part of yourself are you denying? What is stopping you from letting it loose?

3. If you were going to create your own "cool kids" circle, what would it look like? What kind of people would you invite in?

15. Gratitude: Appreciate What Others Have Given You

1. What is a story you could tell on social media about someone who has helped or supported you?

2. How do you think a daily gratitude habit would affect your attitude?

3. When is the last time someone thanked you?
   How did it make you feel?

16. Resilience: Bounce Back Stronger

1. What problem seems insurmountable to you
   right now? Are you trying to avoid an action that
   would solve it?

2. Why do most people give up instead of fighting
   for their dreams?

3. Who is someone you admire that is resilient?
   What do you think made them that way?

17. Integrity: Do the Right Thing

1. When is the last time you were faced with a
   situation where no one would have found out if
   you fudged your integrity? How did you handle it?

2. Has your conscience ever bothered you because
   you made the wrong decision?

3. Do you think it's possible for someone to fully
   recover another person's trust after they have
   shown a lack of integrity?

18. Forgiveness: Let Go of the Baggage

1. Who is the last person you forgave? Was it difficult?

2. Is there someone you need to ask for forgiveness? What is keeping you from asking?

3. Do you struggle with forgiving yourself? Why?

ABOUT THE AUTHOR

Kent Sanders is the founder of Inkwell Ghostwriting, which helps leaders grow their business through books and other content. He is also the author of *The Artist's Suitcase: 26 Essentials for the Creative Journey* and coauthor of *Performance Driven Giving: The Roadmap to Unleashing the Power of Generosity in Your Life* with David Hancock and Bobby Kipper.

In addition to writing books for himself and his clients, Kent loves to serve other writers. He is the host of *The Daily Writer* podcast, which helps writers cultivate the habits for creative success, and the founder of The Daily Writer Club. He lives just outside of St. Louis and enjoys spending time outdoors with his wife and family.

LET'S CONNECT

✉ Kent@KentSanders.net

🌐 KentSanders.net

🐦 @KentSanders

📷 @KentSanders

📘 kentsanders

💼 kent-sanders

🌐 DailyWriterLife.com

🎙 DailyWriterLife.com/podcast

👥 DailyWriterLife.com/club

📷 @DailyWriterLife

A QUICK FAVOR

Thanks so much for reading *18 Words to Live By.* I hope you enjoyed the book!

May I ask a quick favor? Will you take a moment to leave an honest review for *18 Words to Live By* on Amazon? Reviews are the best way to help others find and purchase the book.

You can visit the link below to share a quick review. I appreciate you!

KentSanders.net/18WordsReview

Made in United States
Orlando, FL
11 April 2022

16750211R00104